OAE 056 School Treasurer

Lily P. Washington

This page is intentionally left blank.

This publication is not endorsed by any third-party organization. Names of exams are trademarks of respected organizations.

High Learning Group

The text of this publication, or any part thereof, may not be reproduced in any manner whatsoever without written permission from High Learning Group.

Printed in the United States of America

The authors, compilers, and publisher make no warranties regarding the correctness or completeness of the content contained in this publication and specifically disclaim all warranties whatsoever. Advice, strategies, and suggestions described may not be suitable for every case. Providing web addresses or other (information) services in this publication does not mean/imply that the author or publisher endorses information or websites. Neither the author nor the publisher shall be liable for damages arising herefrom. The author and publisher shall not be held responsible for any damage resulting herefrom from the information provided. There are no guarantees attached to the publication. The content of this publication is best practices, suggestions, common mistakes, and interpretation, and the author and the publisher are not responsible for any information contained in the publication.

Disclaimer: By using this book, you agree to the following: High Learning Group and any individual/company/organization/group involved in the development of this publication specifically disclaims any liability (whether based on contract, tort, strict liability, or otherwise) for any direct, indirect, incidental, consequential, or special damages arising out of or in any way connected with access to the information presented in this publication, even if High Learning Group and any individual/company/organization/group involved in the development of this publication have been advised of the possibility of such damages.

High Learning Group and any individual/company/organization/group involved in the development of this publication are not responsible for the use of this information. Information provided through this publication holds no warranty of accuracy, correctness, or truth. The author, publisher, compilers, and all other parties involved in this work disclaim all responsibility for any errors contained within this work and from the results of the use of this information.

No individual or institution has permission to reproduce (in any form) the contents of this publication.

No individual or institution has permission to reproduce the contents on any website.

This page is intentionally left blank.

Table of Content

Chapter 1 – Questions 1

Chapter 2 – Answers and Explanations 45

This page is intentionally left blank.

Chapter 1 – Questions

QUESTION 1

The school district is implementing a new financial policy that affects the allocation of funds for extracurricular activities. Some parents are concerned that the policy unfairly impacts certain student groups. How should the School Treasurer address these concerns and protect stakeholders' interests?

- A. Ignore the concerns and proceed with the policy as planned.
- B. Engage with concerned parents, gather feedback, and consider adjustments to the policy as appropriate.
- C. Disregard the policy's impact on specific student groups to avoid conflict.
- D. Allocate additional funds to extracurricular activities without assessing the policy's impact.

Answer:

QUESTION 2

When applying rules and regulations related to school district finances, what should be the School Treasurer's approach?

- A. Bypassing regulations for the sake of efficiency
- B. Selectively applying regulations based on personal preferences
- C. Strictly adhering to all relevant regulations and statutes
- D. Ignoring regulations to accommodate influential stakeholders

Answer:

QUESTION 3

The school district is considering a major procurement contract with a vendor that has a history of regulatory violations. Some board members argue that the vendor's competitive pricing justifies the risk. What is the School Treasurer's role in protecting stakeholders' interests in this situation?

- A. Approve the contract without further evaluation to save costs.
- B. Conduct a thorough due diligence review of the vendor's compliance history and assess the potential risks.
- C. Disregard the vendor's compliance history to secure a favorable deal.
- D. Ignore concerns and proceed with the contract regardless of risks.

Answer:

QUESTION 4

As a School Treasurer, what is one of the key benefits of active participation in local, state, and national professional organizations related to education finance?

- A. Increasing your workload with additional commitments
- B. Networking with colleagues and staying updated on industry best practices
- C. Avoiding interaction with other professionals to maintain independence
- D. Isolating yourself from changes in fiscal policies and regulations

Answer:

QUESTION 5

When advocating for improvements in fiscal policies, laws, and regulations that affect education, what should be the primary motivation for a School Treasurer?

- A. Personal gain and recognition
- B. Promoting the interests of specific stakeholders
- C. Enhancing the financial well-being of the school district and education as a whole
- D. Avoiding involvement in policy advocacy to focus on daily tasks

Answer:

QUESTION 6

The school district is facing budgetary challenges due to changes in state funding policies. As the School Treasurer, what steps should you take to advocate for improvements in fiscal policies that benefit the district while considering the interests of the broader education community?

- A. Focus solely on advocating for changes that benefit the district, ignoring broader education issues.
- B. Engage with local and state policymakers, present data on the district's needs, and collaborate with other districts to advocate for fair funding policies.
- C. Avoid engaging with policymakers and accept the challenges as inevitable.
- D. Advocate for policies that prioritize the district's interests over those of the broader education community.

Answer:

QUESTION 7

When contributing to the professional mentoring and growth of new school treasurers, what should be a primary objective?

- A. Keeping valuable knowledge and experience to oneself
- B. Providing guidance and support to help new treasurers succeed
- C. Competing with new treasurers for career advancement
- D. Discouraging new treasurers from seeking professional growth

Answer:

QUESTION 8

A new school treasurer has joined the district and seeks your guidance for professional growth. What actions should you take to mentor the new treasurer effectively?

- A. Refuse to provide any guidance to maintain your competitive advantage.
- B. Share your experiences, offer advice, and provide opportunities for skill development and networking.
- C. Undermine the new treasurer's efforts to ensure your position remains unchallenged.
- D. Disregard the new treasurer's requests for guidance to avoid any distractions.

Answer

QUESTION 9

What is one of the potential benefits of contributing to the professional mentoring and growth of new school treasurers for the School Treasurer and the education finance community as a whole?

- A. Maintaining a competitive advantage over new treasurers
- B. Promoting an isolated and non-collaborative professional environment
- C. Cultivating a supportive and knowledgeable network of professionals
- D. Excluding new treasurers to protect one's own position

Answer:

QUESTION 10

You are the School Treasurer, and the school district is facing budget constraints. To propose a solution, which of the following steps should you take first?

- A. Cut funding for extracurricular activities.
- B. Analyze current expenditures.
- C. Request additional funding from the state.
- D. Increase property taxes.

Answer:

QUESTION 11

As the School Treasurer, you are tasked with aligning financial policies with school district goals. Which of the following should be your primary focus to ensure alignment?

- A. Reducing teacher salaries.
- B. Implementing a new sports facility.
- C. Allocating funds for academic programs.
- D. Increasing administrative expenses.

Answer:

QUESTION 12

You are implementing new financial procedures in the school district to ensure compliance with legal requirements. What is the most critical factor to consider during this process?

- A. Reducing overall expenses.
- B. Minimizing paperwork for staff.
- C. Adhering to state and federal laws.
- D. Increasing the budget for administration.

Answer:

QUESTION 13

The school district must monitor its financial policies and procedures over time. What is the primary purpose of this ongoing monitoring?

- A. To increase administrative salaries.
- B. To identify areas for cost-cutting.
- C. To ensure compliance and effectiveness.
- D. To reduce funding for extracurricular activities.

Answer:

QUESTION 14

You are faced with a situation where the school district needs to negotiate agreements with teachers' unions while maintaining financial stability. What is the most important consideration in this negotiation process?

- A. Offering the highest possible salaries.
- B. Prioritizing the needs of the school district.
- C. Minimizing negotiations to save time.
- D. Collaborating to find mutually beneficial solutions.

Answer:

QUESTION 15

You are tasked with proposing a plan to align the school district's financial policies with its goal of improving student outcomes. Which of the following steps should be your first priority?

- A. Reducing funding for maintenance and facilities.
- B. Allocating more funds to administrative expenses.
- C. Investing in professional development for teachers.
- D. Increasing the budget for extracurricular activities.

Answer:

QUESTION 16

As the School Treasurer in Ohio, you are responsible for managing public school funding. What is the primary source of local funding for public education in Ohio?

- A. Federal grants
- B. State income tax
- C. Property taxes
- D. Sales tax revenue

Answer:

QUESTION 17

Your school district is considering a new capital improvement project, and you need to recommend a tax levy to fund it. Which type of tax levy is typically used to finance such projects in Ohio?

- A. Emergency levy
- B. Operating levy
- C. Bond levy
- D. Income tax levy

Answer:

QUESTION 18

You are forecasting property values for your school district to estimate tax revenue. What effect does Ohio's House Bill 920 have on property tax levies?

- A. It increases property tax rates.
- B. It decreases property tax rates.
- C. It freezes property tax rates.
- D. It has no impact on property tax rates.

Answer:

QUESTION 19

Your school district needs to estimate the potential revenue from a new income tax levy. What is a key factor to consider when forecasting the revenue from an income tax levy?

- A. The assessed property values
- B. The local sales tax rate
- C. The projected income levels of residents
- D. The federal grant allocation

Answer:

QUESTION 20

You are tasked with recommending a tax levy to support ongoing school operations. Which type of tax levy is most suitable for this purpose in Ohio?

- A. Permanent improvement levy
- B. Emergency levy
- C. Renewal levy
- D. Income tax levy

Answer:

QUESTION 21

Your school district is facing a budget shortfall, and you need to identify additional revenue sources. What type of levy allows school districts in Ohio to respond to financial emergencies?

- A. Income tax levy
- B. Emergency levy
- C. Property tax levy
- D. Sales tax levy

Answer:

QUESTION 22

You are the School Treasurer of a small school district in Ohio. Over the years, the district's student enrollment has steadily declined, leading to decreased state funding. To address this financial challenge, you are considering a tax levy. However, you also want to minimize the financial burden on local residents. Which type of tax levy would be the most appropriate choice in this situation?

- A. Bond levy
- B. Renewal levy
- C. Emergency levy
- D. Income tax levy

Answer:

QUESTION 23

Your school district is planning a major capital project to build a new school facility. As the school treasurer, what should be a critical consideration when identifying a finance team for this project?

- A. Selecting team members based solely on their availability
- B. Ensuring team members have no experience in financial matters
- C. Assembling a diverse team with expertise in finance, construction, and project management
- D. Appointing a single individual to handle all financial aspects of the project

Answer:

QUESTION 24

When analyzing the debt structure for a capital project, what factor should be considered when matching the useful life to the length of debt?

- A. Extending the debt term as long as possible to minimize immediate payments
- B. Aligning the debt term with the expected useful life of the project assets
- C. Keeping the debt term shorter than the useful life to reduce interest costs
- D. Ignoring the useful life as it is not relevant to debt structure

Answer:

QUESTION 25

During the construction of a new school facility, the project experiences cost overruns, and additional funding is needed to complete the project. What financing option should the school treasurer consider to address this situation?

- A. Selling off district-owned assets to generate funds
- B. Increasing property taxes to cover the overruns
- C. Exploring short-term financing options such as issuing notes
- D. Delaying the project until sufficient funds are available

Answer:

QUESTION 26

When considering the sale of bonds as a financing option for a capital asset, what is the primary advantage of using bonds?

- A. Bonds do not require interest payments
- B. Bonds have lower interest rates compared to other financing options
- C. Bonds do not involve any external stakeholders
- D. Bonds do not have a fixed maturity date

Answer:

QUESTION 27

Your school district is considering refinancing existing debt to take advantage of lower interest rates. What should the school treasurer prioritize during the refinancing process?

- A. Focusing solely on extending the maturity date of the debt
- B. Identifying potential cost savings while maintaining a manageable debt structure
- C. Avoiding any changes to the existing debt terms
- D. Refinancing without conducting a thorough analysis of market conditions

Answer:

QUESTION 28

In considering lease options for financing capital assets, what key aspect should the school treasurer evaluate to make an informed decision?

- A. Choosing the longest lease term available to minimize immediate costs
- B. Ensuring that the lease option requires no financial commitment from the school district
- C. Comparing the total costs and obligations associated with different lease options
- D. Avoiding lease options altogether to simplify financial management

Answer:

QUESTION 29

When conducting a risk assessment for a school district, what is a critical step in identifying potential risks?

- A. Ignoring minor risks to focus on major threats
- B. Consulting external experts without involving internal stakeholders
- C. Collaboratively involving various departments and personnel in the assessment
- D. Relying solely on historical data and past incidents for risk identification

Answer:

QUESTION 30

In the context of risk management for school district facilities and assets, what is a key consideration when developing risk mitigation strategies?

   A. Avoiding any investments in risk mitigation to minimize costs
   B. Prioritizing insurance coverage over proactive risk reduction measures
   C. Balancing the cost of mitigation measures with the potential risks and losses
   D. Implementing risk reduction measures without assessing their effectiveness

Answer:

QUESTION 31

Your school district is considering purchasing insurance coverage for a recently acquired property. The insurance broker offers two options: a basic policy with lower premiums and a comprehensive policy with higher premiums. What factors should you consider when making a decision?

   A. Opt for the basic policy to save costs without analyzing specific coverage needs
   B. Choose the comprehensive policy without evaluating the property's unique risks
   C. Evaluate the property's specific risks and insurance needs before deciding on coverage
   D. Reject both insurance options and rely on the district's financial reserves

Answer:

QUESTION 32

When evaluating the benefits of insurance protection for school districts, what is a key advantage of having liability insurance?

   A. Eliminating the need for any risk management practices or preventive measures
   B. Providing financial coverage for legal claims and liabilities arising from accidents or injuries
   C. Guaranteeing complete protection against all potential risks
   D. Reducing insurance premiums for other types of coverage

Answer:

QUESTION 33

In the context of risk exposure faced by school districts, what is a limitation of insurance as the sole risk management strategy?

   A. Insurance can cover all potential risks and eliminate the need for other strategies
   B. Insurance premiums are always cost-effective for school districts
   C. Insurance may not cover all losses, and deductibles or exclusions may apply
   D. Insurance does not require ongoing monitoring and management

Answer:

QUESTION 34

As the school treasurer, you are reviewing insurance options for the school district's transportation fleet. What should you prioritize when selecting insurance coverage for this specific risk?

   A. Choosing the cheapest insurance option to save costs
   B. Assessing the specific risks associated with the transportation fleet and selecting appropriate coverage
   C. Relying on self-insurance and not purchasing any external coverage
   D. Focusing solely on insuring other assets, such as buildings and equipment

Answer:

QUESTION 35

You are the school treasurer of a small rural school district. Your district has recently experienced an increase in vandalism incidents at several school facilities. The superintendent has tasked you with conducting a risk assessment to address this issue. As part of the assessment, you collaborate with the school's security personnel, maintenance staff, and local law enforcement. After a thorough analysis, you identify several potential risks, including inadequate lighting, lack of security cameras, and limited police patrols in the area. What is the most appropriate next step to manage the identified risks?

- A. Purchase a comprehensive insurance policy to cover potential vandalism losses.
- B. Share the risk assessment findings with the school board and recommend implementing security measures such as improved lighting and surveillance.
- C. Ignore the risks, as vandalism incidents are common in the area and may not have significant financial impact.
- D. Request additional funding from the state government to hire additional security personnel.

Answer:

QUESTION 36

Your school district has approved a major capital project to renovate and expand several school buildings. The project is expected to last two years and requires significant funding. As the school treasurer, you are responsible for managing the finances of the project. During the first year of the project, you encounter unexpected cost overruns due to unforeseen construction challenges and increased material costs. The project is at risk of exceeding the budget. What should you consider to manage the financial risks associated with the capital project effectively?

- A. Reduce the scope of the project to stay within the budget.
- B. Seek additional funding from the state government to cover the cost overruns.
- C. Explore short-term financing options, such as issuing bonds, to address the funding gap.
- D. Delay the project until sufficient funds are available.

Answer:

QUESTION 37

You are the school treasurer of a diverse school district, and you have recently discovered that a vendor who provides goods to the district is a close relative of one of the school board members. The vendor's prices are significantly higher than those of other suppliers. What action should you take to uphold ethical conduct and avoid conflicts of interest?

- A. Continue using the vendor since they were recommended by a board member.
- B. Address the issue privately with the board member without taking further action.
- C. Seek competitive bids from multiple vendors and select the most cost-effective option.
- D. Ignore the situation as it does not directly impact your role as treasurer.

Answer:

QUESTION 38

As the school treasurer, you receive a report from an employee indicating suspicions of financial misconduct within the district's finance department. The employee claims that funds may have been misappropriated. What is the most appropriate course of action to address this situation while maintaining professional and ethical standards?

- A. Keep the report confidential and conduct a private investigation.
- B. Ignore the report as it may damage the department's reputation.
- C. Immediately report the suspicions to the appropriate authorities and initiate an internal investigation.
- D. Discuss the concerns with the employee who made the report and leave it at that.

Answer:

QUESTION 39

You are tasked with setting expectations for professional and ethical conduct in your school district. How can you effectively communicate these expectations to all stakeholders, including staff, students, and board members?

- A. Develop a comprehensive code of conduct and share it only with key personnel.
- B. Address ethical conduct only during annual training sessions.
- C. Promote a culture of ethics and integrity through regular communication, training, and visible leadership.
- D. Rely on external consultants to communicate expectations to stakeholders.

Answer:

QUESTION 40

Your school district is in the midst of a contentious negotiation with the teachers' union regarding salaries and benefits. As the school treasurer, you are responsible for financial transparency and ethical conduct. During a negotiation session, a union representative suggests that you provide inaccurate financial data to gain an advantage in the negotiation process. What should be your immediate response to uphold ethical conduct?

- A. Comply with the suggestion to maintain a favorable position in the negotiations.
- B. Discuss the suggestion privately with the union representative to understand their motivations.
- C. Reject the suggestion and make it clear that ethical conduct and transparency are non-negotiable principles for the district.
- D. Report the suggestion to the school board without further discussion.

Answer:

QUESTION 41

As the school treasurer, you want to encourage a culture of integrity and fairness in all financial transactions within the district. What is an effective way to promote these values?

- A. Implement a complex financial approval process to slow down transactions.
- B. Provide financial incentives for employees who achieve high transaction volumes.
- C. Lead by example and emphasize the importance of integrity and fairness in all financial interactions.
- D. Delegate all financial decisions to external consultants to avoid internal conflicts.

Answer:

QUESTION 42

In the event that you encounter a suspected violation of professional and ethical standards within your school district, what is the most appropriate action to take to ensure accountability?

- A. Handle the matter discreetly without involving external parties.
- B. Ignore the violation as long as it does not result in financial losses.
- C. Report the suspected violation through the appropriate channels for investigation.
- D. Address the issue informally with the individuals involved to avoid a formal investigation.

Answer:

QUESTION 43

As the school treasurer, you are committed to personal and professional growth to better serve your school district. You have identified the need to enhance your knowledge and skills in financial forecasting to align with district goals. What is the most effective approach to develop and implement a plan for self-improvement in this specific area?

- A. Attend general financial management workshops and conferences.
- B. Seek guidance from colleagues in other districts without formal training.
- C. Develop a structured Individual Professional Development Plan (IPDP) focused on financial forecasting.
- D. Rely on online forums and social media for self-directed learning.

Answer:

QUESTION 44

To remain current with technology and software relevant to school district financial management, what practice should you prioritize as the school treasurer?

- A. Avoid technology updates to minimize disruptions in the district's financial systems.
- B. Attend technology workshops occasionally to acquire basic skills.
- C. Engage in continuous learning and regular training on relevant technology and software.
- D. Delegate all technology-related responsibilities to IT staff.

Answer:

QUESTION 45

As the school treasurer, you have set a goal to encourage and model internal self-assessment among your finance team members. How can you best promote this practice within your team?

- A. Conduct annual performance evaluations to identify areas of improvement.
- B. Discourage team members from self-assessment to avoid negative self-perception.
- C. Foster an environment of trust and open communication, encouraging self-reflection and self-assessment.
- D. Require team members to complete self-assessment forms without discussion.

Answer:

QUESTION 46

Your school district has recently adopted new financial management software to streamline processes and improve efficiency. As the school treasurer, you need to ensure that you and your team are proficient in using this software. What is the most effective approach to ensure you and your team remain current with the new software?

- A. Provide a one-time training session for the team to learn the basics of the software.
- B. Assign the responsibility of software training to individual team members.
- C. Develop a comprehensive training plan that includes initial training and ongoing support.
- D. Rely on external consultants to handle all aspects of software training.

Answer:

QUESTION 47

As part of your commitment to personal and professional growth, you want to align your development with district and professional standards. What approach should you take to achieve this alignment?

- A. Focus solely on your personal interests and skills without considering district or professional standards.
- B. Attend generic training programs without any specific goals or alignment.
- C. Identify district and professional standards and develop a plan for self-improvement aligned with these standards.
- D. Delegate the responsibility for personal and professional growth to a mentor.

Answer:

QUESTION 48

You are tasked with ensuring your finance team remains current with technology relevant to school district financial management. What is a key benefit of regularly updating technology skills within your team?

- A. Reduced reliance on technology, leading to cost savings.
- B. Improved efficiency and effectiveness in financial management processes.
- C. Increased resistance to technological changes among team members.
- D. Elimination of the need for IT support staff.

Answer:

QUESTION 49

What is the primary responsibility of a School Treasurer when collaborating with the board of education in the development of the school district strategic plan?

- A. Providing input on curriculum design
- B. Managing day-to-day school operations
- C. Offering financial expertise and analysis
- D. Facilitating parent-teacher meetings

Answer:

QUESTION 50

When identifying measurable short- and long-term organizational goals for a school district, which of the following is the most essential consideration?

- A. Meeting the expectations of external stakeholders
- B. Aligning with the latest educational trends
- C. Addressing the unique needs of the student population
- D. Emulating successful strategies from other districts

Answer:

QUESTION 51

In a case where a school district's budget is falling short of supporting its strategic plan, what should the School Treasurer prioritize?

- A. Cutting down on extracurricular activities
- B. Expanding administrative staff
- C. Aligning the budget with strategic priorities
- D. Reducing teacher salaries

Answer:

QUESTION 52

When reporting financial data to facilitate strategic planning, what metric is most relevant for assessing the financial impact of the school district's strategic plan?

- A. Total student enrollment
- B. Annual teacher turnover rate
- C. Budget surplus or deficit
- D. Cafeteria menu options

Answer:

QUESTION 53

A school district's strategic plan emphasizes improving technology infrastructure. However, the current budget cannot accommodate the necessary investments. What should the School Treasurer recommend in this situation?

- A. Delay the technology upgrades until the next budget cycle
- B. Reduce spending on teacher professional development
- C. Seek additional funding through grants or partnerships
- D. Cut funding for arts and sports programs

Answer

QUESTION 54

The school district's strategic plan has led to a substantial budget surplus. What action should the School Treasurer take to ensure responsible financial management?

- A. Allocate the surplus to expand all educational programs equally
- B. Set aside a portion of the surplus as a reserve for emergencies
- C. Increase the salaries of all school district employees
- D. Use the surplus for a one-time celebration event

Answer:

QUESTION 55

When making decisions based on financial data to ensure fiscal responsibility, what should the School Treasurer prioritize?

- A. Maximizing short-term profits
- B. Achieving the strategic goals of the school district
- C. Allocating resources without considering long-term impact
- D. Reducing transparency in financial reporting

Answer:

QUESTION 56

In communicating the school district's financial position to internal and external stakeholders, what is the primary purpose?

- A. Justifying budget cuts to staff and teachers
- B. Demonstrating financial prowess to external funders
- C. Providing transparency and accountability
- D. Concealing financial challenges from the public

Answer:

QUESTION 57

In reporting financial information for school-community relations, which of the following would be the most effective way for the School Treasurer to engage with the community?

- A. Conducting closed-door financial meetings
- B. Sharing complex financial data without context
- C. Offering financial literacy workshops for community members
- D. Limiting financial information access to school staff only

Answer:

QUESTION 58

The school district is facing budget constraints due to declining enrollment. As the School Treasurer, what decision should you consider to address this situation?

- A. Reduce funding for academic programs
- B. Increase spending on extracurricular activities
- C. Explore alternative revenue sources such as partnerships
- D. Cut salaries for all district employees

Answer:

QUESTION 59

The school district's budget is in surplus due to unexpected savings. What action should the School Treasurer take to best communicate this surplus to internal stakeholders?

- A. Keep the surplus discreet to avoid expectations
- B. Allocate the entire surplus to employee bonuses
- C. Communicate the surplus and involve stakeholders in allocation decisions
- D. Use the surplus to fund a lavish staff party

Answer:

QUESTION 60

The school district needs to cut costs without compromising educational quality. What approach should the School Treasurer consider to communicate this budget challenge to external stakeholders effectively?

- A. Downplay the budget challenges to maintain a positive image
- B. Host public meetings to discuss budget challenges and gather input
- C. Increase fees for student services to cover the deficit
- D. Restrict access to financial information for external stakeholders

Answer:

QUESTION 61

The school district has been experiencing declining enrollment, resulting in decreased state funding. As the School Treasurer, you are tasked with addressing this financial challenge. What would be the most strategic approach to communicate this situation to the school board and external stakeholders?

- A. Withhold information until a solution is found to avoid unnecessary panic.
- B. Share the enrollment decline data transparently and proactively with the school board and external stakeholders.
- C. Increase fees for student services to compensate for the funding gap.
- D. Begin staff layoffs immediately to reduce expenses.

Answer:

QUESTION 62

The school district's financial position is stable, with a surplus in the budget. However, there are differing opinions among the school board members on how to allocate the surplus funds. As the School Treasurer, what should be your approach to resolve this situation?

- A. Allocate the surplus according to your own preferences to maintain financial control.
- B. Convene a meeting with the school board to discuss their individual priorities and reach a consensus on the surplus allocation.
- C. Keep the surplus funds discreetly to avoid disagreements among board members.
- D. Use the surplus to fund pet projects favored by the school board president.

Answer:

QUESTION 63

The school district's financial reports indicate a steady increase in revenue from community partnerships and donations. However, some community members are concerned about the school district's motives for accepting these funds. How should the School Treasurer address these concerns?

- A. Ignore the concerns as they are unfounded and do not warrant a response.
- B. Issue a public statement reassuring the community that the funds are used exclusively to benefit students and enhance educational programs.
- C. Halt accepting any further community donations to avoid controversy.
- D. Use the additional funds to increase salaries for district administrators.

Answer:

QUESTION 64

When considering short-term financial instruments for managing school district debt, what is the primary benefit of using Tax Anticipation Notes (TANs) over other options?

- A. Lower interest rates
- B. Longer maturity periods
- C. Easier approval process
- D. No need for repayment

Answer:

QUESTION 65

In managing school district debt, what should be the main consideration when deciding to issue long-term general obligation bonds?

- A. Maximizing short-term cash flow
- B. Meeting immediate budgetary needs
- C. The long-term impact on the district's debt service and fiscal health
- D. Avoiding debt altogether

Answer

QUESTION 66

The school district is experiencing financial strain and considering borrowing funds through a long-term bond issue. However, this decision is met with resistance from some community members who are concerned about the increased debt burden. What steps should the School Treasurer take to communicate the necessity and benefits of this bond issuance to the community?

- A. Ignore community concerns and proceed with the bond issuance as planned.
- B. Host closed-door meetings with a select group of community members to address their concerns privately.
- C. Organize public town hall meetings to provide detailed information on the need for the bond issuance and its long-term benefits.
- D. Cancel the bond issuance to avoid controversy.

Answer:

QUESTION 67

When implementing an accounting system for a school district, what is the primary purpose of fund accounting?

- A. Simplifying financial reporting
- B. Combining all revenue and expenses into a single account
- C. Tracking funds separately to ensure proper use and compliance
- D. Minimizing the number of account codes

Answer:

QUESTION 68

Which of the following account codes would be most appropriate for tracking funds designated for school facility maintenance and repairs?

- A. General Fund (GF)
- B. Food Services Fund (FSF)
- C. Capital Projects Fund (CPF)
- D. Transportation Fund (TF)

Answer

QUESTION 69

The school district is considering implementing a new accounting system, and there is a debate about the appropriate use of account codes. Some board members want to simplify the codes to minimize complexity, while others emphasize the need for detailed tracking. What approach should the School Treasurer advocate for in this situation?

   A. Advocate for simplifying the account codes to reduce administrative burden.
   B. Support detailed account codes to enhance transparency and accountability.
   C. Ignore the debate and proceed with the current account code system.
   D. Eliminate account codes altogether to streamline the accounting process.

Answer:

QUESTION 70

When determining the useful life of capital assets in a school district, what should the School Treasurer consider as the most critical factor?

   A. Budget constraints and cost-saving measures
   B. The manufacturer's suggested lifespan
   C. Legal requirements and regulations
   D. The asset's physical condition and maintenance history

Answer:

QUESTION 71

In the context of capital asset disposition, what is the primary goal for a school district?

   A. Maximizing profit from asset sales
   B. Minimizing the time and effort required for disposal
   C. Ensuring compliance with legal and environmental regulations
   D. Disposing of assets regardless of their condition

Answer:

QUESTION 72

The school district owns several aging school buses that require extensive repairs. The debate among the school board members is whether to repair or replace these buses. What factors should the School Treasurer consider when providing recommendations for this decision?

   A. Focus solely on the cost of repairs and replacement buses.
   B. Consider the age of the buses, their maintenance history, and long-term operating costs.
   C. Replace all buses without assessing repair options.
   D. Disregard the environmental impact of replacing buses.

Answer:

QUESTION 73

Which of the following best describes the purpose of a robust maintenance program for school district capital assets?

   A. To eliminate all repair costs entirely
   B. To extend the life of assets and reduce repair expenses
   C. To allocate more funds to other areas of the budget
   D. To avoid reporting asset information to external stakeholders

Answer:

QUESTION 74

The school district has a limited budget and must prioritize which capital assets to include in its maintenance program. What criteria should the School Treasurer use to determine which assets to prioritize for maintenance?

   A. Age of assets and aesthetic condition
   B. Asset usage and compliance with regulatory requirements
   C. Random selection to distribute maintenance efforts equally
   D. Size of assets and popularity among staff

Answer:

QUESTION 75

When developing a financial strategy for maintaining capital assets, what should the School Treasurer consider as the primary financial objective?

   A. Allocating the smallest possible budget to maintenance
   B. Deferring maintenance to minimize short-term costs
   C. Ensuring the long-term financial sustainability of the assets
   D. Increasing expenditures on non-asset-related programs

Answer:

QUESTION 76

When developing insurance policies for a school district, what is the primary consideration for compliance with legal requirements?

   A. Minimizing insurance coverage to reduce costs
   B. Maximizing insurance coverage to eliminate risks
   C. Balancing coverage to meet legal minimums while managing risks
   D. Ignoring legal requirements and focusing on cost savings

Answer:

QUESTION 77

In the context of risk management for school district fleets, what is the primary goal when implementing safety measures?

   A. Eliminating all accidents and incidents
   B. Reducing the frequency and severity of accidents
   C. Ignoring safety measures to cut costs
   D. Placing blame on individual drivers for accidents

Answer:

QUESTION 78

The school district is considering whether to purchase cyber insurance to protect against potential cyber threats. Some board members argue that the cost of cyber insurance is too high. What factors should the School Treasurer consider when making a recommendation on cyber insurance?

   A. The cost of insurance premiums as the sole factor in the decision
   B. The likelihood and potential impact of cyber threats on the district
   C. The assumption that the district will never face a cyber threat
   D. The availability of funds for other non-security-related programs

Answer:

QUESTION 79

When evaluating the financial implications of workers' compensation programs, what should the School Treasurer prioritize?

A. Minimizing workers' compensation claims at all costs
B. Balancing workers' compensation costs with employee safety and support
C. Reducing workers' compensation premiums to the lowest possible level
D. Ignoring workers' compensation programs as they are unrelated to financial matters

Answer:

QUESTION 80

The school district has experienced a significant increase in liability insurance premiums due to multiple recent claims. What should the School Treasurer recommend to address this issue?

A. Cancel the liability insurance policy to save costs
B. Investigate the root causes of the claims and implement preventive measures
C. Ignore the increase in premiums as it is a normal occurrence
D. Transfer all liability risks to individual employees

Answer:

QUESTION 81

When analyzing the financial implications of school safety measures, what should be the primary focus?

A. Cutting safety budgets to save costs
B. Ensuring the safety of students and staff
C. Ignoring safety measures to allocate funds elsewhere
D. Maximizing the district's insurance coverage

Answer:

QUESTION 82

The school district has recently experienced a series of property damage incidents, resulting in increased property insurance premiums. The board is concerned about the rising costs and wants immediate action. As the School Treasurer, what steps should you take to address this situation?

A. Recommend canceling the property insurance policy to reduce premiums.
B. Initiate an in-depth analysis of the property damage incidents and identify preventive measures.
C. Ignore the incidents and accept the rising premiums as a cost of doing business.
D. Shift the responsibility for property damage claims to individual school sites.

Answer:

QUESTION 83

The school district is exploring the purchase of a comprehensive liability insurance policy to protect against potential lawsuits and claims. The premiums for this policy are substantial, and some board members are concerned about the cost. What factors should you consider when making a recommendation on liability insurance?

A. Purchase the policy without further evaluation to ensure comprehensive coverage.
B. Evaluate the district's risk exposure, legal history, and potential financial impact of lawsuits.
C. Disregard the need for liability insurance to allocate funds to other programs.
D. Opt for the cheapest liability insurance policy available to save costs.

Answer:

QUESTION 84

The school district is implementing a cybersecurity program to protect sensitive student and staff data. As the School Treasurer, you are tasked with overseeing the program's financial aspects. The cybersecurity program has a budget overrun due to the need for additional security measures. Some board members suggest cutting the cybersecurity budget to allocate funds to other pressing needs. What is the most prudent course of action?

   A. Cut the cybersecurity budget to allocate funds elsewhere and address immediate needs.
   B. Seek additional funding sources to cover the cybersecurity program's budget overrun.
   C. Ignore the budget overrun and proceed with the program as planned.
   D. Reevaluate the cybersecurity program to identify cost-effective measures while maintaining data security.

Answer:

QUESTION 85

When implementing school district policies, what is the primary responsibility of the School Treasurer to ensure unbiased and consistent application?

   A. Tailoring policies to suit the preferences of individual stakeholders
   B. Applying policies selectively based on personal beliefs
   C. Adhering to policies consistently and fairly
   D. Ignoring policies to accommodate influential stakeholders

Answer:

QUESTION 86

In a case where a school district is facing allegations of financial impropriety, what is the School Treasurer's role in protecting stakeholders' interests?

   A. Suppressing information to avoid negative publicity
   B. Conducting an impartial internal investigation and reporting findings transparently
   C. Blaming external factors to divert attention from the allegations
   D. Refusing to cooperate with external audits or reviews

Answer:

QUESTION 87

You are the School Treasurer in a suburban Ohio school district with aging school buildings. The district has identified the need for significant capital improvements to ensure the safety and functionality of its facilities. To finance these improvements, you must recommend a tax levy to the school board. Which type of tax levy would best suit your goal of financing capital improvements while spreading the cost over time?

   A. Permanent improvement levy
   B. Emergency levy
   C. Bond levy
   D. Income tax levy

Answer:

QUESTION 88

You are the School Treasurer for a rural Ohio school district that heavily relies on property tax revenue. Due to a recent economic downturn in the area, many residents are struggling financially, and there is a concern about increasing property tax rates. Which approach should you consider to address this situation and generate additional revenue for the district while minimizing the impact on residents?

   A. Increase the property tax rate to compensate for lower property values.
   B. Implement an income tax levy to diversify revenue sources.
   C. Request additional state funding to cover the budget shortfall.
   D. Convert an existing renewal levy into a permanent improvement levy.

Answer:

QUESTION 89

You are the School Treasurer tasked with managing the school district's investments. Which of the following is the most critical factor when developing an investment policy for the district?

A. Maximizing short-term returns
B. Complying with federal tax regulations
C. Following the investment preferences of school board members
D. Prioritizing investments with the highest risk-reward ratio

Answer:

QUESTION 90

Your school district aims to generate investment income to support educational programs. Which of the following investment strategies is most suitable for achieving this objective?

A. Investing in high-risk stocks
B. Keeping all funds in low-yield savings accounts
C. Diversifying investments across various asset classes
D. Concentrating investments in a single asset class

Answer:

QUESTION 91

Your school district is evaluating potential investment providers. Which factor should be a top consideration when selecting an investment provider?

A. The provider's past performance in unrelated industries
B. The provider's fees and charges
C. The provider's location
D. The provider's political affiliations

Answer:

QUESTION 92

You are reviewing investment parameters for your school district's funds. What should be a key limitation to ensure the safety of invested funds?

A. Investing a large portion of funds in speculative ventures
B. Diversifying investments across multiple providers
C. Maintaining a high level of liquidity
D. Allowing investments with minimal oversight

Answer:

QUESTION 93

Your school district has received a significant windfall, and you need to make investment decisions to maximize returns. What principle should guide your investment decisions in this situation?

A. Invest all funds in high-risk, high-reward assets
B. Diversify investments to spread risk
C. Keep all funds in low-yield, secure investments
D. Allocate all funds to a single investment provider for convenience

Answer:

QUESTION 94

You are responsible for overseeing student activity programs and their associated funds in your school district. What is the primary purpose of these programs' policies and procedures?

- A. To maximize revenue generation for the school district
- B. To ensure compliance with state and federal tax regulations
- C. To safeguard and transparently manage student activity funds
- D. To provide financial incentives to students

Answer:

QUESTION 95

You are the School Treasurer, and your district is in the process of purchasing new classroom supplies. Which of the following is a critical practice related to purchasing procedures that ensures accountability?

- A. Approving your own purchase requisitions
- B. Allowing teachers to purchase supplies independently
- C. Segregation of duties between requisitioning and approving purchases
- D. Bypassing the competitive bidding process

Answer:

QUESTION 96

Your school district is considering a significant technology purchase. As the School Treasurer, what is your primary responsibility in this purchasing process?

- A. Evaluating the technical specifications of the products
- B. Selecting the vendor with the lowest price
- C. Ensuring compliance with procurement policies and regulations
- D. Negotiating contracts with suppliers

Answer:

QUESTION 97

Your school district has received a grant to upgrade its facilities. You need to initiate a purchasing process for construction services. Several vendors have expressed interest in the project. What is the first step you should take to initiate the purchasing process for construction services in compliance with purchasing principles?

- A. Immediately select a vendor based on your prior experience
- B. Request informal proposals from all interested vendors
- C. Create a detailed project scope and request formal bids
- D. Approve the purchase without seeking competitive bids

Answer:

QUESTION 98

You are responsible for overseeing the purchase of textbooks for the upcoming academic year. What is a critical factor to consider when selecting a textbook supplier?

- A. The supplier's marketing materials
- B. The supplier's willingness to provide free samples
- C. The alignment of textbooks with the curriculum standards
- D. The supplier's location

Answer:

QUESTION 99

Your school district is considering a bulk purchase of laptop computers for students. To achieve cost-efficiency, which purchasing approach should you consider?

A. Purchasing individual laptops from different suppliers
B. Implementing a competitive bidding process
C. Approving the purchase without seeking competitive bids
D. Allowing each school to independently purchase laptops

Answer:

QUESTION 100

Your school district has identified a need for a new security system for all school buildings. The safety of students and staff is a top priority. You are tasked with overseeing the purchase process for this security system. What is the most critical consideration when directing the purchasing process for the security system?

A. Choosing a vendor with the lowest cost
B. Prioritizing the fastest installation timeline
C. Ensuring the security system meets the district's safety requirements
D. Selecting the vendor with the longest warranty period

Answer:

QUESTION 101

As the School Treasurer, you are responsible for ensuring compliance with relevant laws and regulations. What is the primary source of legal guidance for your district's financial operations in Ohio?

A. Local school board policies
B. Federal court decisions
C. Ohio Revised Code (ORC) and Ohio Administrative Code (OAC)
D. Internal Revenue Service (IRS) codes

Answer:

QUESTION 102

Your school district is negotiating a new collective bargaining agreement with the teachers' union. One of the key points of contention is salary adjustments. The district is facing budget constraints. Which of the following should you prioritize to ensure compliance with relevant legal and contractual provisions during these negotiations?

A. Offering a salary increase above what the district can afford
B. Complying with the terms outlined in the existing collective bargaining agreement
C. Ignoring federal statutes to reduce costs
D. Relying solely on local school board policies

Answer:

QUESTION 103

You are reviewing your school district's financial reports, and you notice a potential discrepancy in the application of generally accepted accounting principles (GAAP). What should be your immediate course of action?

A. Ignore the discrepancy since it's a minor issue
B. Notify the school board and external auditors
C. Make adjustments to the reports without documentation
D. Seek guidance from federal statutes

Answer:

QUESTION 104

Your school district is considering a major construction project financed by bonds. To ensure compliance with legal and contractual provisions, which entity should you consult for guidance on the issuance of bonds?

- A. Local school board
- B. The U.S. Department of Education
- C. Ohio Department of Education
- D. State legislature

Answer:

QUESTION 105

Your school district has received a substantial federal grant for a special education program. The grant comes with specific reporting requirements to the funding agency. What is your primary responsibility as the School Treasurer regarding the federal grant's compliance with reporting requirements?

- A. Hire additional staff to handle the reporting
- B. Ensure accurate and timely reporting as required by the grant
- C. Delay reporting until the end of the fiscal year
- D. Rely on board policies to determine reporting timelines

Answer:

QUESTION 106

Your school district has identified a potential conflict between federal statutes and state regulations related to student data privacy. What should be your immediate course of action to address this conflict?

- A. Ignore the conflict and continue with current practices
- B. Seek legal counsel to interpret the conflicting provisions
- C. Comply only with federal statutes, disregarding state regulations
- D. Notify the local school board for resolution

Answer:

QUESTION 107

You are the School Treasurer of a medium-sized school district in Ohio. The district has received a federal grant for a STEM (Science, Technology, Engineering, and Mathematics) program. The grant comes with strict reporting requirements and mandates that funds be used solely for STEM-related initiatives. After the grant is awarded, you discover that a portion of the grant funds has been inadvertently allocated for general school operations due to an administrative error. The district is already facing budget constraints. What should be your immediate course of action to address this situation in compliance with relevant legal and regulatory provisions?

- A. Use the misallocated funds to cover the budget shortfall
- B. Notify the federal grant agency about the error and request guidance
- C. Keep the error confidential to avoid potential consequences
- D. Allocate the misallocated funds to other STEM-related initiatives

Answer:

QUESTION 108

You are the School Treasurer for a small rural school district in Ohio. The district has a longstanding contract with a local supplier for school cafeteria services. The contract, which is governed by state procurement laws, is up for renewal. However, you have received a proposal from a new supplier offering more competitive pricing and improved services. The existing supplier is a significant employer in the community and has provided reliable service for years. Switching to the new supplier would result in job losses for the current cafeteria staff. What is your primary responsibility in this situation to ensure compliance with relevant legal and contractual provisions while making the best decision for the district?

 A. Renew the contract with the existing supplier to protect local jobs
 B. Select the new supplier based on cost savings and improved services
 C. Notify the school board to make the final decision
 D. Delay the decision until a later date

Answer:

QUESTION 109

You are the School Treasurer in a diverse school district in Ohio. The district is in the process of implementing a new student information system (SIS) to improve administrative efficiency and data management. The selected SIS vendor, however, has a reputation for not fully complying with student data privacy regulations in other states. Your district's legal team has raised concerns about the potential risk of non-compliance with federal and state student data privacy laws if you proceed with this vendor. What should be your immediate course of action to address this situation in compliance with relevant legal and regulatory provisions while ensuring the district's data privacy?

 A. Proceed with the selected vendor, as they are the most cost-effective option
 B. Consult with the district's legal team to thoroughly assess the vendor's compliance
 C. Ignore the concerns and trust the vendor's assurances of compliance
 D. Seek guidance from the U.S. Department of Education

Answer:

QUESTION 110

As the School Treasurer, you are responsible for hiring a new finance manager for your school district. Which of the following steps should be your first priority in the recruitment process?

 A. Reviewing resumes and applications
 B. Conducting background checks on candidates
 C. Defining the job requirements and qualifications
 D. Conducting interviews with candidates

Answer:

QUESTION 111

Your school district is experiencing high turnover among teachers due to job dissatisfaction. This has a negative impact on students and the overall work environment. You want to address this issue by enhancing teacher job satisfaction. What organizational development principle should you prioritize to improve teacher job satisfaction?

 A. Increasing the number of mandatory staff meetings
 B. Implementing a performance-based bonus system
 C. Enhancing communication and collaboration among staff
 D. Reducing teacher salaries to allocate funds for other initiatives

Answer:

QUESTION 112

You are responsible for evaluating the performance of your finance team members. What should be the primary focus of performance evaluations in a school finance department?

- A. Assessing personal characteristics of team members
- B. Measuring the number of hours worked by team members
- C. Evaluating team members' job-related skills and competencies
- D. Assigning performance ratings based on team members' seniority

Answer:

QUESTION 113

Your school district has introduced a new policy to promote a positive work environment. The policy includes measures to prevent workplace harassment and bullying. However, you receive a complaint from a staff member alleging harassment by a colleague. What is your immediate responsibility as the School Treasurer to address this complaint in compliance with the new policy and relevant regulations?

- A. Ignore the complaint unless it escalates further
- B. Conduct an impartial investigation into the complaint
- C. Inform the accused colleague about the complaint
- D. Advise the complainant to handle the matter independently

Answer:

QUESTION 114

Your school district is undergoing a reorganization, and you need to delegate authority effectively to ensure smooth operations. Which delegation principle is essential for maintaining a positive, safe, and professional work environment?

- A. Delegating all tasks to a single team member for efficiency
- B. Delegating tasks based solely on seniority
- C. Delegating tasks that match team members' skills and abilities
- D. Delegating tasks without clear instructions

Answer:

QUESTION 115

Your school district has implemented a productivity enhancement program to improve the efficiency of administrative staff. As part of this program, you need to monitor the performance of personnel closely. Which monitoring technique would be most appropriate for this situation to enhance productivity while maintaining a positive work environment?

- A. Implementing strict micromanagement of tasks
- B. Conducting periodic performance reviews and feedback sessions
- C. Reducing salaries to motivate staff to work harder
- D. Assigning all tasks to a single staff member for efficiency

Answer:

QUESTION 116

As the School Treasurer, you are tasked with analyzing student population data over multiple years to determine trends. What is the primary benefit of analyzing this data for a school district?

- A. Identifying opportunities for reducing teacher salaries
- B. Predicting future changes in the student population
- C. Increasing district revenue through fundraising
- D. Demonstrating compliance with state budget regulations

Answer:

QUESTION 117

Your school district has experienced a decline in student enrollment over the past three years, leading to reduced state funding. You are tasked with identifying factors driving this trend. What should be your primary approach to identify the factors driving the decline in student enrollment and revenues?

- A. Reducing school programs and services to align with lower enrollment
- B. Collaborating with local businesses to increase funding
- C. Analyzing historical enrollment data and conducting surveys
- D. Implementing across-the-board budget cuts

Answer:

QUESTION 118

You are reviewing the school district's expenditure trends over the past five years. What key financial indicator should you monitor to identify potential issues with fiscal sustainability?

- A. The total number of students enrolled
- B. The average teacher salary
- C. The amount spent on extracurricular activities
- D. The ratio of expenditures to revenues

Answer:

QUESTION 119

Your school district has observed a steady increase in property tax revenue over the past three years due to rising property values in the community. To make informed decisions about budget allocations, you need to understand the driving factors behind this revenue trend. What should be your first step in identifying the factors driving the increase in property tax revenue?

- A. Reducing expenditures to maximize the surplus
- B. Conducting a property value assessment
- C. Analyzing historical property tax data and economic trends
- D. Requesting additional state funding to offset property tax revenue

Answer:

QUESTION 120

Your school district has experienced a decline in state funding due to changes in government policy. What is a critical step in understanding the impact of this decline on the district's finances?

- A. Reducing teacher salaries to compensate for the funding gap
- B. Conducting a comprehensive review of state funding regulations
- C. Increasing local property taxes to make up for the loss
- D. Implementing across-the-board budget cuts

Answer:

QUESTION 121

Your school district has observed an increase in expenditures related to special education services over the past two years. To address this trend, you need to identify the specific factors driving the increase. What should be your primary approach to identify the factors driving the increase in special education expenditures?

- A. Reducing funding for special education programs
- B. Requesting additional federal funding for special education
- C. Collaborating with special education staff and analyzing student data
- D. Implementing across-the-board budget cuts

Answer:

QUESTION 122

Your school district is facing budgetary challenges due to declining enrollment and increased operational costs. As the School Treasurer, you are tasked with identifying financial issues and proposing solutions. What is the most appropriate first step in this situation?

- A. Cut funding for extracurricular activities to save costs.
- B. Conduct a thorough financial analysis to identify specific budgetary issues.
- C. Request additional funding from the state government.
- D. Implement a hiring freeze for all non-essential positions.

Answer:

QUESTION 123

The school board is considering launching a new after-school program, and they want to ensure it aligns with the district's financial goals. What data should you prioritize in assessing the feasibility of this program?

- A. Historical enrollment data for the past five years.
- B. Student and parent surveys on potential interest in the program.
- C. Average per-student expenditure in the district.
- D. The number of teachers available to staff the program.

Answer:

QUESTION 124

There is a disagreement within the school board regarding the allocation of funds for technology upgrades versus hiring additional teachers. As the School Treasurer, how can you help resolve this conflict?

- A. Advocate for technology upgrades to enhance educational resources.
- B. Suggest increasing the overall budget to accommodate both needs.
- C. Conduct a cost-benefit analysis of both options to provide data-driven insights.
- D. Avoid involvement in the conflict to maintain neutrality.

Answer:

QUESTION 125

The school district's financial reports show a significant increase in energy costs over the past year. What is the most appropriate action for you to take as the School Treasurer?

A. Immediately cut energy consumption by reducing heating and cooling.
B. Investigate the reasons behind the increase in energy costs.
C. Request additional funds from the state government to cover the expenses.
D. Postpone all non-essential expenditures to offset the energy costs.

Answer:

QUESTION 126

As the School Treasurer, you are responsible for collecting and utilizing financial data to assist in program development. Which of the following financial reports would be most useful for evaluating the effectiveness of a new reading program implemented in the district?

A. Monthly payroll records for teaching staff.
B. Annual budget projections for the upcoming fiscal year.
C. Quarterly revenue and expenditure statements.
D. Yearly standardized test scores for students in reading.

Answer

QUESTION 127

The school district is considering a major construction project to expand facilities due to an increasing student population. What process should be followed to ensure sound financial decision-making for this project?

A. Seek input from parents and teachers on the necessity of the project.
B. Hire a construction firm without a competitive bidding process to expedite the project.
C. Conduct a feasibility study, including cost estimates and funding sources.
D. Request additional funding from the state government to cover construction costs.

Answer:

QUESTION 128

Your school district has a significant budget deficit, and the school board is considering various cost-cutting measures. One proposal is to reduce funding for arts programs. As the School Treasurer, what should be your approach to this proposal?

A. Support the reduction in arts program funding to prioritize core academic subjects.
B. Advocate for a comprehensive budget analysis to identify alternative cost-saving measures.
C. Suggest increasing taxes to maintain funding for arts programs.
D. Immediately implement the proposed reduction to address the deficit.

Answer:

QUESTION 129

The school district is preparing its annual budget, and you want to ensure it aligns with state laws and district policies. What should you prioritize when reviewing the budget proposal?

A. Allocating funds for a new technology upgrade.
B. Ensuring compliance with state-mandated funding requirements.
C. Increasing discretionary funds for individual school principals.
D. Implementing across-the-board salary increases for all staff.

Answer:

QUESTION 130

Your school district is experiencing a decline in enrollment, which may impact future revenues. How can you proactively manage this situation in the budget planning process?

A. Immediately reduce staffing levels to align with decreased enrollment.
B. Advocate for increased property taxes to compensate for the enrollment decline.
C. Develop a five-year revenue forecast considering various enrollment scenarios.
D. Postpone all capital improvement projects until enrollment stabilizes.

Answer:

QUESTION 131

The school board is considering a proposal to increase teacher salaries significantly. To support this decision, what financial modeling and planning approach should you recommend?

A. Approve the salary increase without detailed analysis to boost teacher morale.
B. Base the decision on historical salary trends without considering long-term sustainability.
C. Conduct a thorough analysis of the budget impact and consider the long-term financial sustainability.
D. Seek external grants to cover the cost of the salary increase.

Answer:

QUESTION 132

Your school district is in the early stages of the budget cycle, and you are responsible for setting important timelines. What is a critical step to ensure a smooth budget process?

A. Rush the budget process to meet deadlines set by the state.
B. Allow individual schools to set their own budget timelines.
C. Establish clear communication channels and deadlines for budget submissions.
D. Delay the budget process until all financial data is available.

Answer:

QUESTION 133

The school district relies heavily on state funding, and there is uncertainty about potential changes in state budget allocations. How can you prepare for this uncertainty in your budget planning?

A. Ignore the uncertainty and proceed with the budget as usual.
B. Reduce reliance on state funding by seeking alternative revenue sources.
C. Request additional funding from the state preemptively.
D. Develop contingency plans that account for various funding scenarios.

Answer:

QUESTION 134

You are the School Treasurer for a small rural school district facing declining enrollment and an annual budget deficit. The school board is considering a proposal to consolidate two underutilized elementary schools into one, which could potentially save costs. However, this would mean longer commutes for some students and the loss of a community focal point. What should your approach be in this situation?

A. Support the consolidation to immediately reduce operating expenses.
B. Advocate for a comprehensive cost-benefit analysis considering the impact on students, parents, and the community.
C. Propose increasing property taxes to maintain both schools.
D. Recommend closing one school without further analysis to address the deficit.

Answer:

QUESTION 135

Your school district relies heavily on state funding, and there are rumors of potential cuts in the state budget. To prepare for possible funding reductions, what steps should you take as the School Treasurer?

   A. Ignore the rumors and proceed with the budget as planned.
   B. Request a significant increase in local property taxes to offset potential cuts.
   C. Develop multiple budget scenarios, including those with reduced state funding, to identify areas for cost-saving.
   D. Seek additional grants from the state government to maintain current funding levels.

Answer:

QUESTION 136

Your school district has received a substantial one-time grant for improving technology infrastructure. The grant specifies that the funds must be used within the fiscal year. However, you believe that a long-term technology plan would be more beneficial for the district. What should your approach be in managing this grant?

   A. Spend the entire grant within the fiscal year to meet the grant's requirements.
   B. Use a portion of the grant for immediate needs and allocate the rest for a long-term technology plan.
   C. Return the grant funds as they do not align with the district's long-term goals.
   D. Invest the entire grant in long-term technology projects without considering immediate needs.

Answer:

QUESTION 137

What is the primary purpose of developing and implementing school district capital asset policies?

   A. To increase taxes and generate additional revenue for the district.
   B. To provide guidance on the valuation, depreciation, and classification of capital assets.
   C. To reduce expenditures on maintenance and repairs.
   D. To eliminate all capital assets from the district's financial records.

Answer:

QUESTION 138

Your school district is planning to construct a new gymnasium. What should be a key consideration when developing a plan for the construction of this capital asset?

   A. Bypass the bidding process to expedite construction.
   B. Seek contributions from parents and students to fund the project.
   C. Develop a comprehensive plan that includes bidding requirements and project timelines.
   D. Hire contractors without assessing their qualifications.

Answer:

QUESTION 139

Your school district recently acquired a new building for administrative offices. How should this asset be classified in the financial records?

   A. As a current liability.
   B. As an intangible asset.
   C. As a capital asset.
   D. As an operating expense.

Answer:

QUESTION 140

What is the purpose of including depreciation in the financial statements of a school district?

- A. To increase the reported value of capital assets.
- B. To decrease the reported value of capital assets.
- C. To encourage the acquisition of more capital assets.
- D. To avoid compliance with accounting standards.

Answer:

QUESTION 141

Your school district is planning to acquire new school buses. What should you prioritize to ensure compliance with bidding requirements for this capital asset purchase?

- A. Award the contract to a preferred vendor without competitive bidding.
- B. Develop clear specifications for the buses and advertise the bidding opportunity.
- C. Avoid involving multiple vendors to simplify the acquisition process.
- D. Skip the bidding process to expedite the acquisition.

Answer:

QUESTION 142

Your school district is facing budget constraints and is considering selling a piece of unused land to generate revenue. What accounting treatment should you apply to this land?

- A. Record it as an operating expense.
- B. Record it as a capital asset.
- C. Exclude it from the financial records.
- D. Record it as a current liability.

Answer:

QUESTION 143

Your school district is considering outsourcing its transportation services to a private company to reduce costs. What is the primary financial consideration in this decision?

- A. Ensuring students have a consistent and reliable transportation experience.
- B. Minimizing the direct costs of operating the transportation services.
- C. Expanding the district's in-house transportation staff.
- D. Maintaining the status quo without exploring alternatives.

Answer:

QUESTION 144

The school board is exploring options to improve technology services for students. You are tasked with assessing the fiscal impact of upgrading the district's technology infrastructure. What should be a key factor in your analysis?

- A. The potential impact on student engagement and learning outcomes.
- B. The availability of state grants to fund technology upgrades.
- C. The desire to maintain the existing technology infrastructure.
- D. The reduction of staff training costs.

Answer:

QUESTION 145

The school district is experiencing a budget shortfall, and the school board is considering reducing maintenance, grounds, and custodial services to address the deficit. What should you prioritize in evaluating this proposal?

- A. Eliminating these services to reduce costs immediately.
- B. Assessing the potential long-term consequences of reduced maintenance services.
- C. Requesting additional funding from the state government.
- D. Outsourcing these services to a private contractor without further analysis.

Answer:

QUESTION 146

The school district provides free breakfast and lunch to all students as part of its food services program. The school board is considering whether to continue this program due to budget constraints. What should be a key consideration in this decision?

- A. The potential increase in student attendance and academic performance.
- B. The availability of federal funding for food services.
- C. The desire to maintain the status quo without exploring alternatives.
- D. The need to cut all food services to address the budget shortfall.

Answer:

QUESTION 147

The school district's technology services have been outsourced to a third-party provider, and the contract is up for renewal. As the School Treasurer, what should be your primary consideration when negotiating the renewal terms?

- A. Ensuring the district has complete control over all technology services.
- B. Minimizing costs without evaluating the quality of service.
- C. Evaluating the effectiveness of the current technology services provider.
- D. Renewing the contract without any negotiation.

Answer:

QUESTION 148

The school district has outsourced its custodial services to a private company. There have been complaints from parents and staff about the cleanliness of the schools. What action should you take as the School Treasurer to address this issue?

- A. Terminate the contract with the custodial services provider immediately.
- B. Conduct a thorough evaluation of the custodial services provider's performance.
- C. Ignore the complaints and maintain the status quo to save costs.
- D. Request additional funding from the state government to address cleanliness concerns.

Answer:

QUESTION 149

How can political and legislative changes affect school district finances and operations?

- A. They have no impact on school district finances and operations.
- B. They can introduce new funding sources and regulations.
- C. They solely focus on student academic performance.
- D. They lead to immediate budget cuts.

Answer

QUESTION 150

New state legislation mandates a reduction in class sizes, which will require hiring additional teachers. However, the school district is already facing budget constraints. What should be your approach as the School Treasurer?

- A. Refuse to comply with the new legislation to save costs.
- B. Seek additional funding from the state government to cover the hiring expenses.
- C. Evaluate the budget to identify cost-saving measures and potential reallocations.
- D. Cut funding for extracurricular activities to allocate resources for hiring teachers.

Answer:

QUESTION 151

How can school districts proactively navigate political trends that may impact their finances?

- A. By avoiding all involvement in politics.
- B. By closely aligning with the views of the current administration.
- C. By engaging in strategic advocacy and staying informed about policy changes.
- D. By reducing funding for education programs to maintain financial stability.

Answer:

QUESTION 152

A new political trend in your state emphasizes increasing funding for vocational education programs. What should be your role as the School Treasurer in response to this trend?

- A. Ignore the trend and focus on traditional academic programs.
- B. Advocate for increased funding for vocational education programs.
- C. Reduce vocational program funding to allocate resources elsewhere.
- D. Request additional funding for all programs, ignoring the trend.

Answer:

QUESTION 153

How can changes in political leadership, such as a new governor or mayor, impact school district finances?

- A. They have no impact on school district finances.
- B. They can lead to changes in funding priorities and policies.
- C. They result in immediate budget cuts.
- D. They guarantee increased funding for education.

Answer:

QUESTION 154

The state legislature is considering a bill that would increase funding for early childhood education programs but reduce funding for high school extracurricular activities. What should you consider when providing input on this legislation as the School Treasurer?

- A. Advocate for increasing funding for high school extracurricular activities.
- B. Support the bill as it prioritizes early childhood education.
- C. Request additional funding from the state to cover both areas.
- D. Refuse to provide input on the legislation.

Answer:

QUESTION 155

You need to present the annual budget report to the school board. What is the most important consideration for tailoring your communication to this specific audience?

- A. Using technical jargon to demonstrate expertise.
- B. Providing only high-level summary information.
- C. Ensuring clarity and transparency in presenting complex financial data.
- D. Making the presentation as brief as possible to save time.

Answer:

QUESTION 156

What is a key skill for effective collaboration with external stakeholders, such as parents, community members, and school support groups?

- A. Maintaining a closed-door policy to protect sensitive information.
- B. Actively listening to their concerns and feedback.
- C. Ignoring external stakeholder input to focus on internal matters.
- D. Avoiding all forms of communication with external stakeholders.

Answer:

QUESTION 157

You need to write a report on the financial impact of a proposed school expansion project for the superintendent. What is the primary consideration when choosing the format for this report?

- A. Using a highly technical format with financial jargon.
- B. Prioritizing brevity and omitting detailed financial data.
- C. Selecting a format that is clear and easily understandable.
- D. Including personal anecdotes to make the report more engaging.

Answer:

QUESTION 158

What is a critical strategy for collaborating effectively with the board of education as a School Treasurer?

- A. Avoiding involvement in the board's decision-making process.
- B. Presenting financial information without context or explanations.
- C. Providing regular updates and explanations on financial matters.
- D. Limiting communication with the board to formal meetings only.

Answer:

QUESTION 159

The school district is facing a budget crisis, and you need to communicate the situation to parents and community members at a town hall meeting. What communication approach should you prioritize in this situation?

- A. Delivering a one-way, top-down message without soliciting input.
- B. Engaging in open dialogue, actively listening to concerns, and providing solutions.
- C. Avoiding the topic of the budget crisis to prevent panic.
- D. Presenting complex financial data without explanations.

Answer:

QUESTION 160

What is a fundamental skill for collaborating effectively with internal stakeholders, such as school district staff and administrators?

- A. Avoiding all forms of communication to maintain a hierarchical structure.
- B. Ignoring the input and ideas of internal stakeholders.
- C. Encouraging open communication and valuing input from staff and administrators.
- D. Implementing decisions without seeking feedback from internal stakeholders.

Answer:

QUESTION 161

In a situation where a discrepancy is discovered during an internal audit of a school department's financial records, what should the School Treasurer do to ensure compliance with audit procedures?

- A. Immediately report the discrepancy to the local media to maintain transparency.
- B. Notify the school department head and initiate an internal investigation.
- C. Conceal the discrepancy until a full external audit can be conducted.
- D. Ignore the discrepancy as it may be a minor error.

Answer:

QUESTION 162

Which of the following is a critical step in reporting school district revenues, expenditures, and fund balances accurately and timely to local, state, and federal agencies?

- A. Providing estimated figures to meet reporting deadlines.
- B. Ensuring that financial data is presented in a clear and understandable format.
- C. Delaying the reporting process until all data is completely error-free.
- D. Reporting only to local agencies and omitting state and federal reporting.

Answer:

QUESTION 163

During an external audit, the auditors identify several instances of non-compliance with financial regulations in a school building. What is the School Treasurer's primary responsibility in this situation?

- A. Immediately fire all staff involved in the non-compliance.
- B. Document the findings and work with the auditors to develop corrective action plans.
- C. Ignore the audit findings and continue with regular operations.
- D. Notify the auditors that their findings are incorrect.

Answer:

QUESTION 164

In the context of school district financial reporting, what is the purpose of an internal audit?

- A. To report financial information to local, state, and federal agencies.
- B. To identify and correct financial irregularities within the school district.
- C. To distribute funds among various school departments.
- D. To conduct an annual external audit.

Answer:

QUESTION 165

When handling sensitive school district records, what is the most effective way for the School Treasurer to ensure data security and compliance with Ohio open-government laws?

- A. Share all records with the public to maintain transparency.
- B. Implement robust data encryption and access controls.
- C. Store all records in paper format to prevent digital breaches.
- D. Limit access to records only to senior administrators.

Answer:

QUESTION 166

In the context of analyzing school district employment contracts, what is the primary responsibility of the School Treasurer?

- A. Negotiating contracts with employee unions.
- B. Ensuring compliance with contractual compensation arrangements.
- C. Managing the school district's social media accounts.
- D. Overseeing curriculum development.

Answer:

QUESTION 167

The school district has received a request for public records under Ohio's open-government laws. The request includes sensitive financial data. What should the School Treasurer do in response to this request?

- A. Deny the request to protect the confidentiality of financial data.
- B. Immediately release all requested records without review.
- C. Review the request, redact confidential information, and provide non-confidential records.
- D. Ignore the request as it does not pertain to the School Treasurer's role.

Answer:

QUESTION 168

What is the significance of analyzing collective bargaining agreements in the context of school district management?

- A. To determine the school district's curriculum requirements.
- B. To negotiate teacher salaries with employee unions.
- C. To ensure compliance with contractual obligations related to employment terms.
- D. To establish the school district's budget for extracurricular activities.

Answer:

QUESTION 169

You are the School Treasurer, and your district is considering implementing a new technology program to enhance student learning. The program's estimated cost is $100,000, and it is expected to benefit both students and teachers. The school board has allocated a budget of $150,000 for educational initiatives this year. What should you do?

A. Approve the technology program as it falls within the allocated budget.
B. Reject the technology program due to budget constraints.
C. Seek additional funding sources to cover the program's cost.
D. Delay the decision until next year's budget allocation.

Answer:

QUESTION 170

As the School Treasurer, you're tasked with evaluating the cost-effectiveness of a new extracurricular program aimed at improving student engagement. The program's initial cost is $10,000, and it has been running for one year. You gather data indicating a significant increase in student attendance and enthusiasm. However, the program also requires a yearly maintenance cost of $5,000. What is the most appropriate action?

A. Continue funding the program as the benefits outweigh the costs.
B. Discontinue the program due to the ongoing maintenance cost.
C. Increase the program's budget to expand its reach.
D. Allocate funds to a different, more cost-effective initiative.

Answer:

QUESTION 171

Your school district is experiencing declining enrollment, leading to reduced funding from the state. As a School Treasurer, you're tasked with making budget adjustments. Which approach is most aligned with effective financial management?

A. Cut spending across all programs and departments proportionally.
B. Analyze the impact of declining enrollment on various programs and prioritize cuts based on their effectiveness and importance.
C. Request additional funding from the state to offset the enrollment decline.
D. Implement a hiring freeze and reduce staff salaries to maintain program funding.

Answer

QUESTION 172

A neighboring school district has successfully implemented a cost-saving initiative by utilizing renewable energy sources to power their facilities. Your school district is interested in exploring similar options to reduce operational costs. What is the first step you should take as the School Treasurer?

A. Approve the implementation of renewable energy sources immediately.
B. Conduct a feasibility study to assess the potential cost savings and environmental impact.
C. Seek funding from the state to support renewable energy projects.
D. Consult with energy experts to determine the best renewable energy source.

Answer:

QUESTION 173

Your school district is planning to upgrade its technology infrastructure to enhance online learning capabilities. You have received two proposals from different vendors. Vendor A offers a comprehensive solution at a lower cost, while Vendor B provides a more advanced system at a higher price. How should you approach this decision?

- A. Choose Vendor A to save costs and stay within the budget.
- B. Select Vendor B to ensure the best technology for students, even if it exceeds the initial budget.
- C. Seek additional funding to accommodate Vendor B's proposal.
- D. Evaluate both proposals in terms of their impact on student learning and long-term cost-effectiveness.

Answer:

QUESTION 174

Your school district has been experiencing budget deficits for several years. To address this issue, you are considering implementing a cost-sharing program with neighboring districts for certain noninstructional services. What should be your primary consideration when evaluating this option?

- A. Implement the cost-sharing program immediately to reduce deficits.
- B. Ensure that the cost-sharing program does not compromise the quality of services provided to students.
- C. Seek additional funding from the state to eliminate budget deficits.
- D. Explore outsourcing noninstructional services to private companies instead.

Answer:

QUESTION 175

As the School Treasurer, you are responsible for placing a tax levy on the ballot to fund critical educational programs. What is the significance of understanding the election dates and filing deadlines in this process?

- A. Understanding election dates and filing deadlines is unnecessary when placing tax levies on the ballot.
- B. It ensures that the tax levy proposal is presented to voters at the appropriate time.
- C. Election dates and filing deadlines are only relevant for state-level tax proposals, not school districts.
- D. Election dates and filing deadlines are primarily the responsibility of the school board, not the School Treasurer.

Answer:

QUESTION 176

You are tasked with explaining the difference between appropriations and expenditures in the budget process. What is the primary distinction between these two financial terms?

- A. Appropriations refer to the money allocated in the budget, while expenditures are the actual funds spent.
- B. Appropriations and expenditures are interchangeable terms in the budgeting process.
- C. Appropriations represent the amount of revenue generated, while expenditures signify budgetary constraints.
- D. Expenditures are the initial budget allocations, and appropriations reflect the final budget after adjustments.

Answer:

QUESTION 177

Your school district is planning to propose a tax levy to fund a new technology initiative. However, you are unsure about the procedures for placing the tax levy on the ballot. What should you prioritize in this situation?

- A. Proceed with the tax levy proposal and figure out the procedures later.
- B. Consult legal counsel to ensure compliance with election regulations.
- C. Delegate the responsibility of understanding the procedures to another department.
- D. Delay the tax levy proposal until the next fiscal year to allow for more time to research the procedures.

Answer:

QUESTION 178

You are presented with two budget proposals for the upcoming fiscal year: one emphasizes increasing funding for student extracurricular activities, and the other focuses on improving classroom resources. How should you approach this budget decision?

A. Allocate funds equally between both proposals to maintain balance.
B. Prioritize funding for student extracurricular activities to enhance student engagement.
C. Allocate funds based on the potential long-term impact on student success.
D. Reject both proposals and maintain the current budget.

Answer:

QUESTION 179

As the School Treasurer, you're responsible for managing the school district's fixed assets. Why is it essential to implement depreciation practices for these assets?

A. Depreciation practices are unnecessary for fixed assets as they hold their value over time.
B. Depreciation practices help track the historical cost and value of assets accurately.
C. Depreciation practices can only be applied to liquid assets, not fixed assets.
D. Depreciation practices are primarily the responsibility of the maintenance department.

Answer:

QUESTION 180

Your school district utilizes an inventory management system to monitor and control supplies. What is the primary benefit of such a system?

A. It eliminates the need for physical inventory counts.
B. It reduces the cost of purchasing supplies.
C. It provides real-time visibility into inventory levels and usage.
D. It allows for automatic supply replenishment.

Answer:

QUESTION 181

A vendor offers a significant discount on a supply order to your school district in exchange for preferential treatment in future contracts. How should you, as the School Treasurer, respond to this situation?

A. Accept the discount to save the district money and prioritize cost-effectiveness.
B. Reject the discount to maintain ethical procurement practices.
C. Seek legal counsel to determine the legality of the vendor's offer.
D. Consult with the school board before making a decision.

Answer:

QUESTION 182

Your school district is considering implementing a new inventory management system to improve efficiency. How should you evaluate the cost-effectiveness of this system?

A. Implement the system immediately to benefit from increased efficiency.
B. Assess the system's upfront cost and determine if it fits within the budget.
C. Consult with other school districts that have implemented similar systems.
D. Delay the decision until the next fiscal year to allocate funds for the system.

Answer:

QUESTION 183

You discover that a member of your procurement team has violated the code of purchasing and procurement ethics by accepting gifts from a vendor. What should be your immediate course of action?

- A. Ignore the violation as long as it does not impact procurement decisions.
- B. Conduct an internal investigation to gather evidence of the violation.
- C. Report the violation to the appropriate authorities and follow legal procedures.
- D. Warn the team member privately to avoid future ethical breaches.

Answer:

QUESTION 184

As the School Treasurer, you are part of a committee responsible for making staffing decisions. The district is facing budget constraints, and you need to determine which positions to retain. Which factor should be a top priority when making these decisions?

- A. Seniority and years of service.
- B. The cost of salary and benefits for each position.
- C. The popularity of individual staff members among students and parents.
- D. The alignment of each position with district goals and priorities.

Answer:

QUESTION 185

Your school district is committed to providing high-quality professional learning opportunities for all personnel. What should be the primary consideration when designing professional development programs?

- A. The availability of external trainers and consultants.
- B. The convenience of scheduling sessions during regular school hours.
- C. The specific needs and goals of the personnel participating.
- D. The budget allocated for professional development.

Answer:

QUESTION 186

Your school district is planning a series of professional learning sessions for teachers. To maximize the impact of these sessions, what strategy should you employ during the design phase?

- A. Schedule the sessions during school breaks to ensure full attendance.
- B. Include a wide range of topics to cater to diverse interests.
- C. Incorporate opportunities for collaborative learning and application.
- D. Focus solely on theoretical concepts to enhance teachers' knowledge.

Answer:

QUESTION 187

Your school district has limited funds available for professional development. How should you prioritize the allocation of these funds?

- A. Allocate an equal amount of funds to each school in the district.
- B. Prioritize funds for high-performing schools to maintain their success.
- C. Distribute funds based on the specific professional development needs of each school.
- D. Allocate the funds based on the number of teachers in each school.

Answer:

QUESTION 188

Your district has implemented a new online professional learning platform for teachers. However, some teachers are hesitant to engage with the platform. What approach should you take to encourage their participation?

- A. Mandate that all teachers complete a certain number of online courses.
- B. Provide incentives, such as certificates or recognition, for active participation.
- C. Ignore the hesitation and let teachers decide whether to use the platform.
- D. Remove the online platform and revert to traditional in-person professional development.

Answer:

QUESTION 189

What is the primary responsibility of the school treasurer as the chief fiscal officer of a school district in Ohio?

- A. Implementing instructional programs
- B. Managing student enrollment
- C. Ensuring financial accountability and reporting
- D. Overseeing transportation services

Answer:

QUESTION 190

In a school district leadership team meeting, the school treasurer is presented with a proposal to allocate a significant portion of the budget to a new extracurricular program. What should the treasurer's role be in this situation?

- A. Advocate for the program to gain popularity
- B. Approve the proposal without
- C. Analyze the financial impact and provide fiscal recommendations
- D. Leave the decision to other team members

Answer:

QUESTION 191

As a member of the school district policy review committee, what is one of the school treasurer's key responsibilities?

- A. Leading curriculum development
- B. Managing student discipline
- C. Reviewing and recommending changes to district policies
- D. Organizing parent-teacher conferences

Answer:

QUESTION 192

As the secretary to the board of education, what is a critical duty of the school treasurer in this role?

- A. Preparing lesson plans for teachers
- B. Managing school facilities and maintenance
- C. Recording and maintaining accurate minutes of board meetings
- D. Supervising cafeteria operations

Answer:

QUESTION 193

In a school district facing a significant budget deficit, the superintendent proposes staff layoffs to address the financial shortfall. As the school treasurer, you have reservations about the proposal. What should you do in this situation?

- A. Immediately support the superintendent's proposal to avoid conflict
- B. Refuse to engage in discussions and maintain neutrality
- C. Analyze the financial data, present alternative solutions, and engage in constructive dialogue with the superintendent and the board
- D. Resign from your position to avoid involvement in difficult decisions

Answer:

QUESTION 194

During a board of education meeting, a board member suggests redirecting funds allocated for student textbooks to support a new technology initiative. What should the school treasurer's response be?

- A. Immediately endorse the board member's suggestion
- B. Reject the idea without further discussion
- C. Present a comprehensive analysis of the potential impact on education and budget, highlighting the pros and cons
- D. Leave the decision entirely to the board members

Answer:

QUESTION 195

In preparation for an upcoming school board meeting, the superintendent requests that you provide a comprehensive financial report. While reviewing the financial data, you notice discrepancies in revenue figures from the previous year. What is your most appropriate course of action?

- A. Disregard the discrepancies as minor errors and proceed with the report.
- B. Include the discrepancies in the report but do not investigate further.
- C. Investigate the discrepancies, identify their causes, and report your findings along with the financial report.
- D. Inform the superintendent but keep the discrepancies undisclosed to avoid causing concern.

Answer:

QUESTION 196

When communicating financial statements and budgets to the superintendent and the board of education, what is the primary objective?

- A. Presenting information in a complex manner to demonstrate expertise
- B. Making the data easily understandable to facilitate informed decision-making
- C. Hiding unfavorable financial information to avoid concerns
- D. Delaying the communication of financial information

Answer:

QUESTION 197

As a school treasurer, what technology tools or systems can you utilize to improve the gathering, management, and reporting of school district financial data?

- A. Stick to traditional paper-based record-keeping to ensure security
- B. Explore and implement modern financial management software and databases
- C. Rely solely on handwritten reports to maintain a personal touch
- D. Avoid technology altogether to reduce costs

Answer:

QUESTION 198

In a situation where the school district experiences a sudden drop in enrollment, how should the school treasurer handle the financial reporting?

A. Downplay the enrollment decline in financial reports to avoid causing panic
B. Include the enrollment decline in the reports but provide no analysis or recommendations
C. Analyze the impact of the enrollment decline on the budget and present this analysis in financial reports
D. Keep the enrollment decline information confidential to prevent speculation

Answer:

QUESTION 199

In preparing a financial forecast for the school district, what factors should the school treasurer consider beyond historical financial data?

A. Rely solely on historical data for forecasting accuracy
B. Ignore any economic or demographic changes in the community
C. Take into account economic trends, legislative changes, and future enrollment projections
D. Focus exclusively on short-term financial projections

Answer:

QUESTION 200

You are tasked with securing sensitive financial data for the school district, including student records and financial transactions. What is the most appropriate approach to ensure data security?

A. Store all data on unencrypted personal devices for easy access
B. Share login credentials with colleagues for convenience
C. Implement strict data encryption, access controls, and regular security audits
D. Avoid storing any data, even if it means limited access to important information

Answer:

QUESTION 201

Your school district is facing a temporary cash flow shortage due to delayed state funding. As the school treasurer, what is the most appropriate strategy to manage this situation effectively?

A. Immediately cut funding for non-essential programs and services
B. Delay employee payroll to conserve cash
C. Implement short-term borrowing to cover the funding gap
D. Request additional funding from the board of education

Answer:

QUESTION 202

When preparing a cash flow analysis for the school district, what should be the main focus of the analysis?

A. Projecting future expenses only
B. Estimating revenues without considering expenditures
C. Forecasting both inflows and outflows of cash
D. Ignoring cash flow analysis as it is not essential for school finance

Answer:

QUESTION 203

In order to enhance internal controls related to cash handling, what should be a critical component of the school district's procedures?

- A. Allowing multiple employees to have unrestricted access to cash
- B. Implementing regular reconciliation of cash transactions and bank statements
- C. Conducting cash transactions without any documentation
- D. Keeping cash handling procedures informal and flexible

Answer:

QUESTION 204

During an internal audit of the school district's payroll operations, discrepancies are discovered between reported hours worked and actual hours worked by some employees. What should the school treasurer do in response to this situation?

- A. Ignore the discrepancies to avoid confrontation
- B. Immediately terminate the employees in
- C. Conduct a thorough investigation to identify the cause of the discrepancies and take appropriate corrective actions
- D. Discuss the discrepancies with the affected employees and leave the resolution to them

Answer:

QUESTION 205

When evaluating the school district's purchasing operations, what is a key indicator of effective internal controls?

- A. Lack of documentation for purchase orders and invoices
- B. A single individual responsible for all purchasing decisions
- C. A clear segregation of duties among those involved in the purchasing process
- D. Keeping purchasing procedures flexible with no defined roles

Answer:

QUESTION 206

As the school treasurer, you receive a report from an internal auditor highlighting deficiencies in the school district's cash handling procedures. What should your immediate response be?

- A. Disregard the auditor's findings as they may not be accurate
- B. Take action to address the identified deficiencies and improve internal controls
- C. Avoid discussing the findings with anyone to prevent panic
- D. Terminate the auditor for making critical observations

Answer:

This page is intentionally left blank.

Chapter 2 – Answers and Explanations

QUESTION 1

Answer: B

Explanation: Protecting stakeholders' interests requires engaging with concerned parties, gathering feedback, and making adjustments to policies as needed to address legitimate concerns.

QUESTION 2

Answer: C

Explanation: The School Treasurer should strictly adhere to all relevant regulations and statutes to ensure compliance, transparency, and financial integrity within the school district.

QUESTION 3

Answer: B

Explanation: The School Treasurer's role is to protect stakeholders' interests by conducting a thorough due diligence review of the vendor's compliance history and assessing potential risks before entering into a contract, ensuring responsible decision-making.

QUESTION 4

Answer: B

Explanation: Active participation in professional organizations allows School Treasurers to network with peers, share knowledge, and stay updated on industry best practices, which can enhance their effectiveness in their roles.

QUESTION 5

Answer: C

Explanation: The primary motivation for advocating for fiscal policy improvements should be the betterment of the school district and the education system as a whole, rather than personal gain or specific stakeholder interests.

QUESTION 6

Answer: B

Explanation: Effective advocacy involves engaging with policymakers, presenting data, and collaborating with other districts to advocate for fair funding policies that benefit the district while considering the broader education community.

QUESTION 7

Answer: B

Explanation: The primary objective when contributing to the growth of new school treasurers should be providing guidance and support to help them succeed and develop professionally, rather than hoarding knowledge or discouraging their growth.

QUESTION 8

Answer: B

Explanation: Effective mentoring involves sharing experiences, offering advice, and providing opportunities for skill development and networking to help the new treasurer grow professionally.

QUESTION 9

Answer: C

Explanation: Contributing to the growth of new treasurers fosters a supportive and knowledgeable network of professionals in the education finance community, benefiting both individual treasurers and the field as a whole through collaboration and shared expertise.

QUESTION 10

Answer: B

Explanation: The correct answer is B) Analyze current expenditures. Before making any decisions that may affect students and the community, it's crucial to understand where the current budget is being spent. Analyzing expenditures provides essential information for making informed decisions and identifying areas where cost savings can be achieved.

QUESTION 11

Answer: C

Explanation: The correct answer is C) Allocating funds for academic programs. The primary focus should be on aligning financial policies with the core mission of the school district, which is typically centered around education and academic excellence. Allocating funds for academic programs supports this alignment.

QUESTION 12

Answer: C

Explanation: The correct answer is C) Adhering to state and federal laws. When implementing financial procedures to ensure compliance, the most critical factor is to follow all relevant state and federal laws. This helps the school district avoid legal issues and potential financial penalties.

QUESTION 13

Answer: C

Explanation: The correct answer is C) To ensure compliance and effectiveness. Ongoing monitoring of financial policies and procedures is essential to ensure they are compliant with laws and effective in achieving their intended goals. It helps identify any necessary adjustments to maintain alignment with the district's objectives.

QUESTION 14

Answer: D

Explanation: The correct answer is D) Collaborating to find mutually beneficial solutions. In negotiations with teachers' unions, it's essential to work collaboratively to find solutions that benefit both parties and maintain financial stability. This approach fosters a positive working relationship and promotes the well-being of both teachers and the school district.

QUESTION 15

Answer: C

Explanation: The correct answer is C) Investing in professional development for teachers. To improve student outcomes, investing in the professional development of teachers is crucial. It directly supports the district's goal by enhancing teaching quality and student learning experiences.

QUESTION 16

Answer: C

Explanation: The correct answer is C) Property taxes. In Ohio, the primary source of local funding for public education is property taxes collected by local school districts. Property taxes are a significant contributor to the funding of schools at the local level.

QUESTION 17

Answer: C

Explanation: The correct answer is C) Bond levy. In Ohio, bond levies are commonly used to finance capital improvement projects, such as building or renovating school facilities. These levies are designed to fund specific capital expenditures and are repaid over time.

QUESTION 18

Answer: B

Explanation: The correct answer is B) It decreases property tax rates. House Bill 920 in Ohio is designed to reduce property tax rates as property values increase to prevent property tax windfalls for local governments. It ensures that property taxes remain relatively stable for taxpayers.

QUESTION 19

Answer: C

Explanation: The correct answer is C) The projected income levels of residents. When forecasting revenue from an income tax levy, it's essential to consider the income levels of residents in the district, as the tax is typically based on a percentage of their income. This projection helps estimate potential revenue.

QUESTION 20

Answer: C

Explanation: The correct answer is C) Renewal levy. A renewal levy in Ohio is used to generate funds for the ongoing operations of a school district. It does not increase taxes but renews an existing levy for continued funding.

QUESTION 21

Answer: B

Explanation: The correct answer is B) Emergency levy. In Ohio, an emergency levy can be used by school districts to respond to financial emergencies or unexpected budget shortfalls. It provides a temporary source of additional revenue when needed.

QUESTION 22

Answer: B

Explanation: In this scenario, with declining enrollment and the need to maintain financial stability without increasing the tax burden on local residents, a renewal levy would be the most appropriate choice. A renewal levy allows the district to continue generating funds for ongoing operations without increasing taxes, as it renews an existing levy.

QUESTION 23

Answer: C

Explanation: The correct answer is C) Assembling a diverse team with expertise in finance, construction, and project management. Building a finance team with a range of expertise ensures a comprehensive approach to financing and managing the capital project.

QUESTION 24

Answer: B

Explanation: The correct answer is B) Aligning the debt term with the expected useful life of the project assets. Matching the debt term to the useful life ensures that the debt is repaid as the assets generate benefits, optimizing financial sustainability.

QUESTION 25

Answer: C

Explanation: The correct answer is C) Exploring short-term financing options such as issuing notes. Short-term financing options like notes can provide the necessary funds to cover cost overruns and ensure the timely completion of the project.

QUESTION 26

Answer: B

Explanation: The correct answer is B) Bonds have lower interest rates compared to other financing options. Bonds often have lower interest rates, making them an attractive option for financing capital assets, as they can result in reduced long-term borrowing costs for the school district.

QUESTION 27

Answer: B

Explanation: The correct answer is B) Identifying potential cost savings while maintaining a manageable debt structure. When refinancing, the school treasurer should seek to reduce interest costs while ensuring that the debt structure remains suitable for the district's financial situation.

QUESTION 28

Answer: C

Explanation: The correct answer is C) Comparing the total costs and obligations associated with different lease options. To make an informed decision, the school treasurer should analyze and compare the financial implications of various lease options to choose the most cost-effective and suitable one for the district's needs.

QUESTION 29

Answer: C

Explanation: The correct answer is C) Collaboratively involving various departments and personnel in the assessment. Collaborative involvement ensures a comprehensive examination of risks from different perspectives and helps identify potential threats more effectively.

QUESTION 30

Answer: C

Explanation: The correct answer is C) Balancing the cost of mitigation measures with the potential risks and losses. Effective risk management involves evaluating the cost-effectiveness of mitigation strategies in relation to the potential impact of risks and losses.

QUESTION 31

Answer: C

Explanation: The correct answer is C) Evaluate the property's specific risks and insurance needs before deciding on coverage. It is essential to assess the property's unique risks and requirements to determine the appropriate insurance coverage to protect the district's assets adequately.

QUESTION 32

Answer: B

Explanation: The correct answer is B) Providing financial coverage for legal claims and liabilities arising from accidents or injuries. Liability insurance helps protect school districts from the financial burden of legal claims and liabilities, ensuring that resources are available to address such issues.

QUESTION 33

Answer: C

Explanation: The correct answer is C) Insurance may not cover all losses, and deductibles or exclusions may apply. Insurance policies often have limitations, deductibles, and exclusions, which means that not all losses may be fully covered, necessitating additional risk management strategies.

QUESTION 34

Answer: B

Explanation: The correct answer is B) Assessing the specific risks associated with the transportation fleet and selecting appropriate coverage. It is crucial to evaluate the unique risks related to the transportation fleet and choose insurance coverage that adequately addresses those risks to protect the district's assets and operations.

QUESTION 35

Answer: B

Explanation: While insurance coverage (Option A) is essential, it does not directly address the identified risks. Ignoring the risks (Option C) is not advisable, as it may lead to further incidents and financial losses. Requesting additional funding (Option D) may not be the most immediate solution. The best course of action is to inform the school board of the risks and recommend practical security measures based on the assessment findings (Option B).

QUESTION 36

Answer: C

Explanation: While reducing the project scope (Option A) and seeking additional state funding (Option B) are options, they may not address the immediate financial needs of the project. Delaying the project (Option D) may have consequences and further costs. Exploring short-term financing options, such as issuing bonds (Option C), can provide the necessary funds to cover cost overruns and ensure the timely completion of the project, making it the most suitable choice.

QUESTION 37

Answer: C

Explanation: To uphold ethical conduct and avoid conflicts of interest, it is essential to ensure fair and transparent procurement practices. Seeking competitive bids from multiple vendors (Option C) promotes fairness and cost-effectiveness while mitigating potential conflicts of interest. Options A, B, and D do not address the ethical concern adequately.

QUESTION 38

Answer: C

Explanation: When suspicions of financial misconduct arise, it is crucial to act promptly and ethically. Option C involves reporting the suspicions to the appropriate authorities and initiating an internal investigation, which is consistent with ethical standards and accountability. Options A, B, and D do not appropriately address the seriousness of the situation.

QUESTION 39

Answer: C

Explanation: Effective communication of professional and ethical expectations involves creating a culture of ethics and integrity. Regular communication, training, and visible leadership (Option C) help foster a commitment to ethical conduct among all stakeholders. Options A, B, and D do not promote a holistic approach to ethical expectations.

QUESTION 40

Answer: C

Explanation: Upholding ethical conduct is paramount, especially in negotiations. Option C involves rejecting the suggestion and affirming the district's commitment to ethical conduct and transparency. Options A, B, and D compromise ethical standards in various ways.

QUESTION 41

Answer: C

Explanation: Promoting a culture of integrity and fairness begins with leadership and setting the right example. Option C encourages the treasurer to lead by demonstrating and emphasizing these values. Options A, B, and D do not address the root of the issue effectively.

QUESTION 42

Answer: C

Explanation: Ensuring accountability for suspected violations of professional and ethical standards requires reporting through proper channels for a transparent and objective investigation. Option C aligns with ethical and accountability principles. Options A, B, and D do not promote accountability effectively.

QUESTION 43

Answer: C

Explanation: Developing a structured IPDP (Option C) allows for a systematic approach to self-improvement, ensuring that your professional growth aligns with district goals. Options A, B, and D may not provide a focused and goal-oriented approach to improvement.

QUESTION 44

Answer: C

Explanation: Staying current with technology and software requires continuous learning and regular training (Option C) to adapt to advancements and maximize their potential in financial management. Options A, B, and D do not address the need for ongoing skill development effectively.

QUESTION 45

Answer: C

Explanation: Creating an environment of trust and open communication (Option C) encourages team members to engage in self-reflection and self-assessment voluntarily. This approach promotes personal and professional growth. Options A, B, and D may not foster a positive and constructive atmosphere for self-assessment.

QUESTION 46

Answer: C

Explanation: A comprehensive training plan (Option C) ensures that the team is well-prepared to use the new software effectively. It includes initial training and ongoing support to address any challenges or s that may arise. Options A, B, and D may not provide adequate support for long-term proficiency.

QUESTION 47

Answer: C

Explanation: Aligning personal and professional growth with district and professional standards (Option C) ensures that your development efforts contribute to the overall goals and standards of the school district. Options A, B, and D may not lead to alignment with specific standards.

QUESTION 48

Answer: B

Explanation: Regularly updating technology skills within the team (Option B) enhances efficiency and effectiveness in financial management processes, ultimately benefiting the school district. Options A, C, and D do not align with the goal of improving technology skills.

QUESTION 49

Answer: C

Explanation: The School Treasurer plays a crucial role in providing financial expertise and analysis when collaborating with the board of education to ensure the financial aspects of the strategic plan are sound and sustainable.

QUESTION 50

Answer: C

Explanation: Defining goals that cater to the specific needs and characteristics of the student population is crucial for the success of a school district's strategic plan.

QUESTION 51

Answer: C

Explanation: The School Treasurer should ensure that the budget aligns with the strategic priorities of the school district to achieve the desired goals without compromising essential services or personnel.

QUESTION 52

Answer: C

Explanation: The budget surplus or deficit is a critical financial metric that directly reflects the financial impact of the school district's strategic plan and its sustainability.

QUESTION 53

Answer: C

Explanation: To support the strategic plan's objectives, the School Treasurer should explore external funding sources, such as grants or partnerships, to bridge the budget gap without sacrificing other essential programs.

QUESTION 54

Answer: B

Explanation: It is fiscally responsible to establish a reserve fund to address unexpected financial challenges or emergencies rather than immediately allocating the surplus to other programs or expenses.

QUESTION 55

Answer: B

Explanation: The School Treasurer should prioritize aligning financial decisions with the school district's strategic goals to ensure long-term fiscal responsibility and sustainability.

QUESTION 56

Answer: C

Explanation: Effective communication of the school district's financial position is essential to maintain transparency and accountability to stakeholders, including staff, parents, and the community.

QUESTION 57

Answer: C

Explanation: Engaging the community through financial literacy workshops helps empower community members with the knowledge to understand the district's financial position and build trust.

QUESTION 58

Answer: C

Explanation: Exploring alternative revenue sources, such as partnerships, can help mitigate budget constraints without compromising the quality of academic programs or employee salaries.

QUESTION 59

Answer: C

Explanation: Open communication and involving stakeholders in allocation decisions demonstrate transparency and foster trust among internal stakeholders regarding the surplus.

QUESTION 60

Answer: B

Explanation: Hosting public meetings to discuss budget challenges and gather input from external stakeholders fosters transparency and allows for community involvement in finding solutions to the budget challenges.

QUESTION 61

Answer: B

Explanation: Transparency is key in addressing financial challenges. Sharing the enrollment decline data openly with the school board and external stakeholders allows for collaboration and the exploration of potential solutions, fostering trust and informed decision-making.

QUESTION 62

Answer: B

Explanation: Collaboration and consensus-building are crucial in such situations. Bringing the school board members together to discuss and agree on the surplus allocation ensures that decisions are made collectively and reflect the priorities of the entire board.

QUESTION 63

Answer: B

Explanation: Addressing concerns with transparency and a clear message is essential. Issuing a public statement that assures the community about the purpose of the funds and their positive impact on students and educational programs will help build trust and maintain the support of community partners.

QUESTION 64

Answer: A

Explanation: Tax Anticipation Notes (TANs) often come with lower interest rates compared to other short-term instruments, making them a cost-effective choice for managing temporary cash flow deficits.

QUESTION 65

Answer: C

Explanation: Issuing long-term general obligation bonds should be based on a careful assessment of their long-term impact on the district's debt service and fiscal sustainability, rather than solely meeting immediate budgetary needs.

QUESTION 66

Answer: C

Explanation: Transparent communication through public town hall meetings can help address community concerns, provide essential information, and build support for the necessary bond issuance.

QUESTION 67

Answer: C

Explanation: Fund accounting separates funds to ensure proper tracking, compliance, and accountability, allowing for a clear understanding of how funds are used within the district.

QUESTION 68

Answer: C

Explanation: The Capital Projects Fund (CPF) is typically used to track funds allocated for capital improvements, such as facility maintenance and repairs.

QUESTION 69

Answer: B

Explanation: Detailed account codes are essential for transparency and accountability in financial reporting, allowing for better tracking and understanding of financial transactions within the district.

QUESTION 70

Answer: D

Explanation: The useful life of a capital asset is often determined by its physical condition and maintenance history, as these factors directly impact the asset's ongoing functionality and value.

QUESTION 71

Answer: C

Explanation: The primary goal in capital asset disposition for a school district is to ensure compliance with legal and environmental regulations to avoid potential liabilities.

QUESTION 72

Answer: B

Explanation: When deciding whether to repair or replace assets like school buses, a comprehensive assessment should consider factors such as age, maintenance history, and long-term operating costs, rather than just immediate costs.

QUESTION 73

Answer: B

Explanation: A maintenance program aims to extend the useful life of capital assets and reduce repair expenses over time by preventing major breakdowns and ensuring assets are in good working condition.

QUESTION 74

Answer: B

Explanation: Prioritizing assets for maintenance based on their usage and compliance with regulatory requirements ensures that critical assets are well-maintained and in compliance with necessary standards.

QUESTION 75

Answer: C

Explanation: The primary financial objective of asset maintenance should be to ensure the long-term financial sustainability of the assets, which ultimately reduces long-term costs and extends the assets' useful life.

QUESTION 76

Answer: C

Explanation: Compliance with legal requirements involves striking a balance between meeting minimum insurance requirements mandated by law and effectively managing risks within the school district.

QUESTION 77

Answer: B

Explanation: The primary goal of fleet risk management is to reduce the frequency and severity of accidents, which ultimately leads to improved safety and cost savings.

QUESTION 78

Answer: B

Explanation: The decision to purchase cyber insurance should consider the likelihood and potential impact of cyber threats on the district's financial and operational stability, rather than solely focusing on the cost of premiums.

QUESTION 79

Answer: B

Explanation: The School Treasurer should prioritize balancing workers' compensation costs with employee safety and support, as these programs are essential for both financial stability and employee well-being.

QUESTION 80

Answer: B

Explanation: To address increasing liability insurance premiums, the School Treasurer should recommend investigating the root causes of the claims and implementing preventive measures to reduce future liabilities.

QUESTION 81

Answer: B

Explanation: The primary focus when analyzing the financial implications of school safety measures should be on ensuring the safety of students and staff, as the well-being of the school community is paramount.

QUESTION 82

Answer: B

Explanation: In this scenario, it is crucial to conduct an analysis to understand the causes of the property damage incidents and implement preventive measures. This proactive approach can help reduce future claims and stabilize insurance premiums.

QUESTION 83

Answer: B

Explanation: When considering liability insurance, it is essential to evaluate the district's risk exposure, legal history, and potential financial impact of lawsuits. This assessment ensures that the insurance policy aligns with the district's needs and risk profile.

QUESTION 84

Answer: D

Explanation: In this situation, it is prudent to reevaluate the cybersecurity program to identify cost-effective measures while maintaining data security. Cutting the budget without compromising security is essential to address both immediate needs and long-term data protection.

QUESTION 85

Answer: C

Explanation: The School Treasurer's primary responsibility is to apply policies consistently and fairly, ensuring that they are not influenced by personal biases or external pressures.

QUESTION 86

Answer: B

Explanation: To protect stakeholders' interests, the School Treasurer should conduct an impartial internal investigation and report the findings transparently, ensuring accountability and integrity.

QUESTION 87

Answer: C

Explanation: In this case, a bond levy would be the most suitable choice. Bond levies are commonly used to finance capital improvements and construction projects in Ohio school districts. They allow the district to spread the cost of these improvements over time while providing funds for essential facility upgrades.

QUESTION 88

Answer: B

Explanation: Given the economic challenges and the desire to minimize the impact on residents, implementing an income tax levy would be a suitable approach. This allows the district to diversify its revenue sources and generate funds without increasing the burden on property owners who may be struggling due to declining property values.

QUESTION 89

Answer: B

Explanation: The correct answer is B) Complying with federal tax regulations. When developing an investment policy for a school district, ensuring compliance with federal tax regulations is crucial. Failure to comply can lead to tax penalties and jeopardize the district's financial stability.

QUESTION 90

Answer: C

Explanation: The correct answer is C) Diversifying investments across various asset classes. Diversification helps spread risk and potentially generate investment income while minimizing exposure to the volatility of a single asset class. It is a prudent strategy for school districts seeking investment income.

QUESTION 91

Answer: B

Explanation: The correct answer is B) The provider's fees and charges. When selecting an investment provider, it's essential to consider their fees and charges, as these can significantly impact the returns on investments. Lower fees can lead to better net returns for the school district.

QUESTION 92

Answer: A

Explanation: The correct answer is A) Investing a large portion of funds in speculative ventures. To ensure the safety of invested funds, it's essential to limit exposure to speculative or high-risk ventures. Prudent investment parameters should prioritize safety and liquidity.

QUESTION 93

Answer: B

Explanation: The correct answer is B) Diversify investments to spread risk. Even with a windfall, it's essential to maintain a diversified investment portfolio to spread risk and mitigate the potential for significant losses. Diversification is a fundamental principle of prudent investing.

QUESTION 94

Answer: C

Explanation: The correct answer is C) To safeguard and transparently manage student activity funds. The primary purpose of policies and procedures for student activity programs is to ensure the responsible and transparent management of funds, safeguarding these funds for the benefit of students and the school community.

QUESTION 95

Answer: C

Explanation: The correct answer is C) Segregation of duties between requisitioning and approving purchases. Segregation of duties is a fundamental internal control practice that prevents a single individual from having complete control over the purchasing process. It enhances accountability and reduces the risk of fraud or mismanagement.

QUESTION 96

Answer: C

Explanation: The correct answer is C) Ensuring compliance with procurement policies and regulations. The primary responsibility of the School Treasurer in the purchasing process is to ensure that all procurement activities adhere to the district's established policies and regulations. This includes overseeing competitive bidding processes, contract compliance, and ethical procurement practices.

QUESTION 97

Answer: C

Explanation: The first step in initiating a purchasing process for construction services is to create a detailed project scope and request formal bids. This step ensures transparency and compliance with purchasing principles by allowing multiple vendors to compete based on the same project requirements.

QUESTION 98

Answer: C

Explanation: The correct answer is C) The alignment of textbooks with the curriculum standards. When selecting a textbook supplier, it is critical to consider whether the textbooks align with the curriculum standards and educational goals of the school district. This ensures that the textbooks are suitable for the students' learning needs.

QUESTION 99

Answer: B

Explanation: The correct answer is B) Implementing a competitive bidding process. To achieve cost-efficiency in a bulk purchase, it's essential to implement a competitive bidding process. This allows vendors to submit their best offers, ensuring the district gets the most favorable pricing and terms.

QUESTION 100

Answer: C

Explanation: The most critical consideration when directing the purchasing process for a security system in a school district is ensuring that the system meets the district's safety requirements. Safety and security should be the top priorities, and cost, installation timeline, and warranty should be secondary considerations.

QUESTION 101

Answer: C

Explanation: The correct answer is C) Ohio Revised Code (ORC) and Ohio Administrative Code (OAC). In Ohio, the ORC and OAC are primary sources of legal guidance for school district financial operations. They outline state laws and regulations that school districts must follow.

QUESTION 102

Answer: B

Explanation: During collective bargaining negotiations, it's essential to prioritize compliance with the terms outlined in the existing collective bargaining agreement to ensure legal and contractual compliance. Deviating from these terms without negotiation or proper legal processes can lead to legal disputes.

QUESTION 103

Answer: B

Explanation: The correct answer is B) Notify the school board and external auditors. When you identify a potential discrepancy in the application of GAAP, it's essential to notify the school board and external auditors. This ensures transparency and compliance with financial reporting standards.

QUESTION 104

Answer: C

Explanation: The correct answer is C) Ohio Department of Education. When considering a major construction project financed by bonds, it's essential to consult with the Ohio Department of Education for guidance and to ensure compliance with state-level regulations and legal provisions related to bond issuance.

QUESTION 105

Answer: B

Explanation: The primary responsibility of the School Treasurer regarding federal grant compliance with reporting requirements is to ensure accurate and timely reporting as stipulated by the grant. Timely and accurate reporting is essential for maintaining compliance and securing future grant funding.

QUESTION 106

Answer: B

Explanation: The correct answer is B) Seek legal counsel to interpret the conflicting provisions. When a conflict arises between federal statutes and state regulations, it's essential to seek legal counsel to provide guidance and interpretation. This ensures that the district's actions are legally sound and compliant with both federal and state requirements.

QUESTION 107

Answer: B

Explanation: In this situation, it's essential to prioritize compliance with relevant legal and regulatory provisions. The correct course of action is to notify the federal grant agency about the error and request guidance on how to rectify it. Misusing grant funds for unintended purposes can have serious legal and financial consequences, so transparency and corrective action are crucial.

QUESTION 108

Answer: B

Explanation: In this situation, your primary responsibility is to ensure compliance with relevant legal and contractual provisions while making the best decision for the district. Procurement decisions should prioritize the best interests of the district, which may include cost savings and improved services. While considering the impact on local jobs is important, the decision should align with the district's goals and procurement regulations.

QUESTION 109

Answer: B

Explanation: When faced with concerns about compliance with relevant legal and regulatory provisions, it's essential to consult with the district's legal team to assess the vendor's compliance thoroughly. Data privacy is a critical issue, and the district must prioritize compliance to avoid potential legal consequences. Relying on vendor assurances without a comprehensive legal assessment could pose risks to student data privacy.

QUESTION 110

Answer: C

Explanation: The correct answer is C) Defining the job requirements and qualifications. In the recruitment process, it's essential to first define the job requirements and qualifications to ensure that you attract candidates who meet the specific needs of the position. This step helps streamline the entire hiring process and ensures you select the most suitable candidate.

QUESTION 111

Answer: C

Explanation: Improving teacher job satisfaction can be achieved by enhancing communication and collaboration among staff. When teachers feel connected, supported, and engaged in the school community, they are more likely to be satisfied with their jobs, which can reduce turnover.

QUESTION 112

Answer: C

Explanation: The correct answer is C) Evaluating team members' job-related skills and competencies. Performance evaluations in a school finance department should primarily focus on assessing the job-related skills, competencies, and contributions of team members to ensure they are effectively carrying out their responsibilities.

QUESTION 113

Answer: B

Explanation: In compliance with the new policy and relevant regulations, your immediate responsibility as the School Treasurer is to conduct an impartial investigation into the complaint. This ensures a fair and thorough examination of the situation, allowing you to take appropriate action to address workplace harassment and bullying.

QUESTION 114

Answer: C

Explanation: The correct answer is C) Delegating tasks that match team members' skills and abilities. Effective delegation involves assigning tasks to team members who have the skills and abilities necessary to perform them successfully. This principle ensures that tasks are completed professionally, enhancing the work environment.

QUESTION 115

Answer: B

Explanation: To enhance productivity while maintaining a positive work environment, conducting periodic performance reviews and feedback sessions is the most appropriate technique. This approach provides staff with constructive feedback, opportunities for improvement, and a chance to contribute to their own professional development, which can motivate them to be more efficient and engaged.

QUESTION 116

Answer: B

Explanation: The correct answer is B) Predicting future changes in the student population. Analyzing student population data over multiple years allows the school district to identify trends, which can be used to predict future changes in student enrollment. This is valuable for planning and allocating resources effectively.

QUESTION 117

Answer: C

Explanation: To identify the factors driving the decline in student enrollment and revenues, the primary approach should be to analyze historical enrollment data and conduct surveys. This comprehensive approach can help uncover the root causes of the trend, allowing the district to make informed decisions.

QUESTION 118

Answer: D

Explanation: The correct answer is D) The ratio of expenditures to revenues. Monitoring the ratio of expenditures to revenues is a key financial indicator to assess fiscal sustainability. If expenditures consistently exceed revenues, it can signal potential financial challenges for the district.

QUESTION 119

Answer: C

Explanation: To identify the factors driving the increase in property tax revenue, the first step should be to analyze historical property tax data and economic trends. This analysis can provide insights into the causes of the revenue increase and help guide budget decisions.

QUESTION 120

Answer: B

Explanation: The correct answer is B) Conducting a comprehensive review of state funding regulations. Understanding the impact of a decline in state funding requires a thorough examination of the state funding regulations and policies that led to the funding change. This review can help the district make informed decisions and advocate for necessary adjustments.

QUESTION 121

Answer: C

Explanation: To identify the factors driving the increase in special education expenditures, the primary approach should be to collaborate with special education staff and analyze student data. This collaborative and data-driven approach can help pinpoint the root causes and allow the district to make informed decisions while maintaining the quality of special education services.

QUESTION 122

Answer: B

Explanation: Cutting funding for extracurricular activities or implementing a hiring freeze without understanding the underlying issues can negatively impact the school district. Requesting additional funding should be considered after identifying and communicating the specific financial issues through a comprehensive analysis.

QUESTION 123

Answer: C

Explanation: To support fiscally sound decision-making, it's crucial to consider the financial aspect. Assessing the average per-student expenditure provides insights into the district's budgetary capacity and helps determine if the program can be sustained without straining resources.

QUESTION 124

Answer: C

Explanation: To support decision-making and resolve conflicts, conducting a cost-benefit analysis objectively evaluates the pros and cons of each option. This analysis can guide the school board in making an informed and financially responsible choice.

QUESTION 125

Answer: B

Explanation: Rather than taking hasty actions that may affect the school environment, it's essential to first understand the reasons behind the cost increase. Investigating the root causes will help in addressing the issue effectively and making informed decisions.

QUESTION 126

Answer: D

Explanation: To assess the effectiveness of a reading program, standardized test scores provide direct evidence of student performance. Other financial reports are essential but may not directly measure the program's impact on student outcomes.

QUESTION 127

Answer: C

Explanation: Conducting a feasibility study is a critical step in the decision-making process for a construction project. It assesses the project's viability, estimated costs, and potential funding sources, ensuring that the decision aligns with the district's financial goals and capabilities.

QUESTION 128

Answer: B

Explanation: Rather than making hasty decisions that could impact the quality of education, advocating for a thorough budget analysis allows for the exploration of alternative solutions to address the deficit while considering the broader implications.

QUESTION 129

Answer: B

Explanation: Ensuring compliance with state laws and funding requirements is a fundamental responsibility of the School Treasurer. This helps avoid legal issues and ensures the district's financial stability.

QUESTION 130

Answer: C

Explanation: Developing a five-year revenue forecast with enrollment scenarios allows the district to plan for potential changes in revenue and make informed decisions without immediate staff cuts or excessive tax increases.

QUESTION 131

Answer: C

Explanation: Making significant salary increases should be based on a comprehensive analysis to ensure the district's financial health and sustainability. A thorough examination of the budget impact is essential.

QUESTION 132

Answer: C

Explanation: Clear communication and established deadlines are crucial for coordinating the budget process effectively and ensuring that all stakeholders are aligned with the timeline.

QUESTION 133

Answer: D

Explanation: Given the uncertainty of state funding, it's prudent to develop contingency plans that consider different funding scenarios, ensuring the district can adapt to changing financial conditions.

QUESTION 134

Answer: B

Explanation: Consolidating schools is a complex decision with wide-ranging implications. Advocating for a comprehensive cost-benefit analysis allows for an informed decision that considers the financial impact along with the broader effects on students, parents, and the community.

QUESTION 135

Answer: C

Explanation: To prepare for potential funding reductions, it's essential to develop budget scenarios that account for various funding levels, allowing the district to proactively identify cost-saving measures and maintain financial stability.

QUESTION 136

Answer: B

Explanation: While it's important to meet grant requirements, a balanced approach is beneficial. Using a portion of the grant for immediate needs ensures compliance, and allocating the rest for long-term planning allows the district to make strategic and sustainable technology improvements.

QUESTION 137

Answer: B

Explanation: The development and implementation of capital asset policies are essential to ensure proper accounting, valuation, and depreciation of assets, leading to accurate financial reporting and compliance with accounting standards.

QUESTION 138

Answer: C

Explanation: When planning the construction of a capital asset, it is crucial to have a well-defined plan that includes bidding requirements to ensure a transparent and competitive procurement process, which can result in cost savings and quality control.

QUESTION 139

Answer: C

Explanation: A building used for administrative offices should be classified as a capital asset, as it has a long-term economic benefit and should be recorded on the balance sheet rather than expensed as an operating cost.

QUESTION 140

Answer: B

Explanation: Depreciation is recorded to allocate the cost of capital assets over their useful life, which reduces their reported value on the balance sheet, reflecting their gradual consumption or obsolescence over time.

QUESTION 141

Answer: B

Explanation: To ensure compliance with bidding requirements, it's essential to have clear specifications, advertise the bidding opportunity, and encourage competition among vendors to obtain the best value for the district.

QUESTION 142

Answer: B

Explanation: Unused land should be classified as a capital asset until it is sold, at which point it may be reclassified as a current asset or cash, depending on the transaction. This treatment reflects the asset's long-term value to the district until it is no longer held.

QUESTION 143

Answer: B

Explanation: The primary financial consideration in outsourcing transportation services is to reduce direct operating costs, which can potentially lead to cost savings for the district.

QUESTION 144

Answer: A

Explanation: When assessing the fiscal impact of technology services, it's essential to consider the potential improvement in student engagement and learning outcomes, as these can have long-term financial implications for the district.

QUESTION 145

Answer: B

Explanation: Prioritizing an evaluation of the long-term consequences of reduced maintenance services is crucial to ensure that cost-cutting measures do not lead to more significant financial challenges or negatively impact the school district's infrastructure.

QUESTION 146

Answer: A

Explanation: When evaluating the food services program, it's essential to consider the potential positive impact on student attendance and academic performance, as this can have financial implications for the district, including potential funding based on attendance.

QUESTION 147

Answer: C

Explanation: When negotiating the renewal terms for a technology services contract, it's essential to assess the effectiveness of the current provider to ensure that the district receives value for the services rendered.

QUESTION 148

Answer: B

Explanation: To address cleanliness concerns, it's important to conduct a thorough evaluation of the custodial services provider's performance to determine whether contract terms are being met and if improvements or adjustments are needed. Terminating the contract should be considered only after a comprehensive assessment.

QUESTION 149

Answer: B

Explanation: Political and legislative changes can significantly impact school district finances and operations by introducing new funding sources, regulations, and mandates that require adaptation and compliance.

QUESTION 150

Answer: C

Explanation: When facing new legislative mandates, it's essential to evaluate the budget, identify potential cost-saving measures, and explore reallocations to meet the requirements without compromising other essential programs.

QUESTION 151

Answer: C

Explanation: To proactively navigate political trends, school districts should engage in strategic advocacy efforts and stay informed about policy changes to influence decisions that affect their finances positively.

QUESTION 152

Answer: B

Explanation: Responding to a political trend that emphasizes vocational education programs may involve advocating for increased funding to align with the trend's priorities while maintaining the overall balance of the district's budget.

QUESTION 153

Answer: B

Explanation: Changes in political leadership can result in shifts in funding priorities and policies, which can have a significant impact on school district finances, potentially affecting budget allocations and funding levels.

QUESTION 154

Answer: A

Explanation: To represent the interests of the school district, advocating for increased funding for high school extracurricular activities while supporting early childhood education can help strike a balance between the two priorities.

QUESTION 155

Answer: C

Explanation: When presenting to the school board, it's crucial to communicate complex financial information clearly and transparently to ensure that board members can make informed decisions regarding the budget.

QUESTION 156

Answer: B

Explanation: Effective collaboration with external stakeholders requires active listening to understand their concerns and feedback, fostering positive relationships and addressing their needs.

QUESTION 157

Answer: C

Explanation: When preparing a financial report for the superintendent, it's essential to select a format that is clear and easily understandable, ensuring that the information is accessible and facilitates informed decision-making.

QUESTION 158

Answer: C

Explanation: Effective collaboration with the board of education involves providing regular updates and explanations on financial matters, ensuring transparency and understanding of the district's financial situation.

QUESTION 159

Answer: B

Explanation: In a budget crisis, it's crucial to engage in open dialogue, actively listen to concerns, and provide solutions when communicating with parents and community members to build trust and address their worries effectively.

QUESTION 160

Answer: C

Explanation: Collaborating effectively with internal stakeholders requires encouraging open communication and valuing their input, which can lead to more informed and inclusive decision-making processes within the school district.

QUESTION 161

Answer: B

Explanation: The correct answer is B. The School Treasurer should notify the school department head and initiate an internal investigation when a discrepancy is discovered during an internal audit. This promotes transparency and allows for corrective actions to be taken promptly, ensuring compliance with audit procedures. Options A, C, and D are not appropriate as they do not follow proper procedures for addressing discrepancies.

QUESTION 162

Answer: B

Explanation: The correct answer is B. Ensuring that financial data is presented in a clear and understandable format is crucial for accurate and timely reporting to local, state, and federal agencies. Option A may lead to inaccuracies, option C can cause unnecessary delays, and option D is not compliant with reporting requirements.

QUESTION 163

Answer: B

Explanation: The correct answer is B. The School Treasurer's primary responsibility is to document the findings and work collaboratively with the auditors to develop corrective action plans based on the audit report. Options A, C, and D are not appropriate responses to address non-compliance issues identified during an external audit.

QUESTION 164

Answer: B

Explanation: The correct answer is B. The purpose of an internal audit in school district financial reporting is to identify and correct financial irregularities within the school district. Option A is the purpose of external reporting, option C relates to budgeting, and option D pertains to external auditing.

QUESTION 165

Answer: B

Explanation: The correct answer is B. Implementing robust data encryption and access controls is essential for ensuring data security and compliance with Ohio open-government laws. Option A is not a best practice for sensitive data, option C ignores the benefits of digital recordkeeping, and option D is too restrictive and may hinder necessary access.

QUESTION 166

Answer: B

Explanation: The correct answer is B. The primary responsibility of the School Treasurer in the context of employment contracts is to ensure compliance with contractual compensation arrangements, including salaries, wages, and fringe benefits. Option A relates to negotiations, option C pertains to a different role, and option D is unrelated to employment contracts.

QUESTION 167

Answer: C

Explanation: The correct answer is C. In response to a public records request, the School Treasurer should review the request, redact confidential information, and provide non-confidential records in compliance with Ohio open-government laws. Option A is too restrictive, option B is risky and may violate privacy laws, and option D is not a responsible course of action.

QUESTION 168

Answer: C

Explanation: The correct answer is C. Analyzing collective bargaining agreements is significant to ensure compliance with contractual obligations related to employment terms within the school district. Option A relates to curriculum, option B focuses on negotiations, and option D is unrelated to employment terms.

QUESTION 169

Answer: C

Explanation: While the technology program is beneficial, it's essential to ensure that the budget remains within the allocated amount. Seeking additional funding sources, such as grants or partnerships, is a critical step in managing the financial components to support instructional programs without exceeding the budget.

QUESTION 170

Answer: A

Explanation: The program's positive impact on student engagement justifies its ongoing cost. As a School Treasurer, it's important to recognize the value of programs that yield educational benefits, even if they require maintenance expenses.

QUESTION 171

Answer: B

Explanation: When faced with budget challenges due to declining enrollment, it's essential to make informed decisions by evaluating each program's effectiveness and importance. This approach ensures that resources are allocated efficiently to support instructional and noninstructional programs.

QUESTION 172

Answer: B

Explanation: Before implementing renewable energy sources, it's crucial to conduct a feasibility study to determine the financial viability and environmental impact of such a project. This ensures that the decision is based on data and aligns with long-term financial planning.

QUESTION 173

Answer: D

Explanation: The decision should be based on a comprehensive evaluation of the proposals, considering their impact on student learning and long-term cost-effectiveness. This approach ensures that financial decisions support instructional programs and align with short- and long-term planning.

QUESTION 174

Answer: B

Explanation: While cost-saving measures are essential, it's crucial to prioritize the quality of services provided to students. Ensuring that the cost-sharing program maintains or enhances service quality aligns with the responsibility of managing financial components to support instructional and noninstructional programs.

QUESTION 175

Answer: B

Explanation: Understanding election dates and filing deadlines is crucial for School Treasurers to ensure that tax levy proposals are submitted in a timely manner, allowing voters to consider and approve necessary funding for educational programs.

QUESTION 176

Answer: A

Explanation: Appropriations are the budgeted amounts allocated for various purposes, while expenditures represent the actual funds spent from the budget. Understanding this distinction is essential for effective financial management.

QUESTION 177

Answer: B

Explanation: Placing a tax levy on the ballot involves legal and regulatory requirements. Consulting legal counsel is essential to ensure compliance with election regulations and procedures to avoid potential issues.

QUESTION 178

Answer: C

Explanation: The critical thinking approach involves evaluating the proposals' potential long-term impact on student success and allocating resources accordingly, considering the educational goals and priorities of the school district.

QUESTION 179

Answer: B

Explanation: Depreciation practices are crucial for maintaining accurate financial records and assessing the true value of fixed assets over time, ensuring transparency and proper financial management.

QUESTION 180

Answer: C

Explanation: An inventory management system offers real-time data on inventory levels and usage, helping School Treasurers make informed decisions about reordering supplies, reducing waste, and ensuring items are available when needed.

QUESTION 181

Answer: B

Explanation: Accepting preferential treatment from a vendor in exchange for future contracts can compromise ethical procurement practices. As a School Treasurer, it's essential to prioritize transparency and fairness in procurement decisions.

QUESTION 182

Answer: B

Explanation: Evaluating the upfront cost of the inventory management system in relation to the budget is a critical step in determining its cost-effectiveness. This ensures responsible financial management and alignment with budget constraints.

QUESTION 183

Answer: C

Explanation: Violations of the code of purchasing and procurement ethics should be taken seriously. Reporting the violation to the appropriate authorities and following legal procedures is essential to maintain transparency, integrity, and compliance with ethical standards.

QUESTION 184

Answer: D

Explanation: When making staffing decisions, it is crucial to prioritize positions that align with the district's goals and priorities to ensure that resources are allocated effectively to support the district's mission and objectives.

QUESTION 185

Answer: C

Explanation: Effective professional development programs should be tailored to the specific needs and goals of the personnel involved, ensuring that learning experiences are relevant and beneficial.

QUESTION 186

Answer: C

Explanation: Collaborative learning and application of knowledge are essential elements of effective professional learning. They allow teachers to apply what they've learned in their classroom practice, leading to better outcomes for students.

QUESTION 187

Answer: C

Explanation: Prioritizing funds based on the unique professional development needs of each school ensures that resources are allocated efficiently to address specific challenges and support improvement where it is most needed.

QUESTION 188

Answer: B

Explanation: Providing incentives can motivate teachers to engage with the online professional learning platform, recognize their efforts, and encourage active participation in professional development opportunities.

QUESTION 189

Answer: C

Explanation: The correct answer is C) Ensuring financial accountability and reporting. The school treasurer's primary role is to oversee the financial aspects of the school district, including budgeting, financial reporting, and fiscal accountability.

QUESTION 190

Answer: C

Explanation: The correct answer is C) Analyze the financial impact and provide fiscal recommendations. As a member of the school district leadership team, the treasurer's role is to offer financial expertise and insights to ensure responsible budget decisions.

QUESTION 191

Answer: C

Explanation: The correct answer is C) Reviewing and recommending changes to district policies. The school treasurer's role on the policy review committee involves participating in the review of existing policies and suggesting updates or changes as needed.

QUESTION 192

Answer: C

Explanation: The correct answer is C) Recording and maintaining accurate minutes of board meetings. As the secretary to the board of education, the school treasurer is responsible for documenting board meetings and ensuring that official records are kept accurately.

QUESTION 193

Answer: C

Explanation: The correct answer is C) Analyze the financial data, present alternative solutions, and engage in constructive dialogue with the superintendent and the board. As the chief fiscal officer, it is the treasurer's responsibility to provide financial expertise and explore alternative solutions when facing budgetary challenges.

QUESTION 194

Answer: C

Explanation: The correct answer is C) Present a comprehensive analysis of the potential impact on education and budget, highlighting the pros and cons. The school treasurer should provide a detailed financial analysis to inform the board's decision-making process and ensure responsible financial management.

QUESTION 195

Answer: C

Explanation: The correct answer is C) Investigate the discrepancies, identify their causes, and report your findings along with the financial report. As the school treasurer, it's crucial to ensure the accuracy of financial data and report any discrepancies or issues to maintain transparency and financial integrity.

QUESTION 196

Answer: B

Explanation: The correct answer is B) Making the data easily understandable to facilitate informed decision-making. The primary goal when communicating financial information is to ensure that the superintendent and board members can comprehend the data and make informed decisions based on it.

QUESTION 197

Answer: B

Explanation: The correct answer is B) Explore and implement modern financial management software and databases. Leveraging technology tools can streamline data management, improve accuracy, and enhance reporting capabilities, ultimately benefiting the school district's financial management.

QUESTION 198

Answer: C

Explanation: The correct answer is C) Analyze the impact of the enrollment decline on the budget and present this analysis in financial reports. The school treasurer should provide a thorough analysis of significant changes in enrollment to help stakeholders understand the financial implications and potential actions required.

QUESTION 199

Answer: C

Explanation: The correct answer is C) Take into account economic trends, legislative changes, and future enrollment projections. Effective financial forecasting involves considering a range of factors, including economic and legislative changes, to create a more accurate and informed financial outlook.

QUESTION 200

Answer: C

Explanation: The correct answer is C) Implement strict data encryption, access controls, and regular security audits. Protecting sensitive financial data is paramount, and the best approach is to use encryption, access controls, and regular security assessments to safeguard the information from unauthorized access or breaches.

QUESTION 201

Answer: C

Explanation: The correct answer is C) Implement short-term borrowing to cover the funding gap. Short-term borrowing can provide the necessary liquidity to manage cash flow shortages without disrupting essential services or delaying employee payroll.

QUESTION 202

Answer: C

Explanation: The correct answer is C) Forecasting both inflows and outflows of cash. Cash flow analysis should consider both the sources of cash (revenues) and the uses of cash (expenditures) to provide a comprehensive view of the district's financial health.

QUESTION 203

Answer: B

Explanation: The correct answer is B) Implementing regular reconciliation of cash transactions and bank statements. Regular reconciliation helps detect discrepancies and ensures that cash handling procedures are accurate and accountable.

QUESTION 204

Answer: C

Explanation: The correct answer is C) Conduct a thorough investigation to identify the cause of the discrepancies and take appropriate corrective actions. It is essential to investigate such discrepancies to ensure payroll accuracy and address any potential issues.

QUESTION 205

Answer: C

Explanation: The correct answer is C) A clear segregation of duties among those involved in the purchasing process. Effective internal controls require a separation of duties to prevent conflicts of interest and enhance accountability in purchasing operations.

QUESTION 206

Answer: B

Explanation: The correct answer is B) Take action to address the identified deficiencies and improve internal controls. It is the treasurer's responsibility to address internal control weaknesses and ensure that proper procedures are in place to handle cash effectively and securely.

Milton Keynes UK
Ingram Content Group UK Ltd.
UKHW030632161023
430697UK00014B/550